Walking in faith and life-changing stories of redemption ... and transparency, Wendi gracefully shares how her 'yes' to God led their family to adopt both internationally and locally. *Not Forgotten* is a story of heartbreak, healing, and hope. Through each turned page, your heart will be opened, your faith will be inspired, and you will see proof of God's faithfulness. In the pages of this book, you will embark on an authentic journey from orphan to sonship. You will see how God was near in every situation. God truly keeps His promise never to leave us.

—**Bob Goff,** *New York Times* bestselling author, speaker, coach and dreamer, author of several books including *Love Does* and *Everybody, Always.*

Not Forgotten is a powerful journey of redemption. Wendi Cross shares raw and vulnerable stories of loss, grief, and abandonment that ultimately lead to God's love and faithfulness. Through the trials and triumphs of an adopted son, Neb, Wendi shows us the transformative power of God's presence in the darkest of times. This book will touch the hearts of parents and young adults who have faced difficult challenges, reminding them that they are never alone. It's a testament to the fact that even in the midst of pain, God is near, offering healing and redemption. *Not Forgotten* will inspire you to believe in the unbelievable and find hope in God's promises.

—**Prince Amukamara,** former NFL Cornerback, and a member of the New York Giants Super Bowl XLVI Championship team.

In her book, *Not Forgotten,* Wendi Cross connects the reader to her story right from the start. Whether you are an adoptive family, a foster family, or you have no children, this glimpse into surrendering to God will encourage you to press into God's best for you, even in the face of hardship. Wendi's use of storytelling makes this an inviting read you won't want to put down.

—**Shontell Brewer,** Host of *Standing in the Grey Podcast,* author of *Missionary Mom.*

This book feels as if the Cross family has invited us in to share their raw and powerful journey of family, God's family. A family that goes the distance for one another, loves unconditionally and never leaves anyone behind. A family that is rooted in faith and trust that is without borders. *Not Forgotten* is the beautiful and impactful story of one boy learning to transcend from broken to whole. This heartfelt story is written with truth and grace and will encourage readers long after the final page is turned. It has inspired my family and I know it will captivate your family's heart as well.

—**Maci Carlile,** co-founder of *Soul Sisters Blog* and RN, BSN, PPHN.

Not Forgotten offers hope to those of us waiting on a miracle. Hope that not only can the miracle come, but also that tiny miracles are happening all around us—if only we are willing to open our eyes and hearts to them. Wendi Cross allows us to peek into the real world of brokenness, love, and redemption. God's love and faithfulness are woven throughout this story and remind all of us that He is good all the time.

—**Lovelyn Palm,** Founder of Shine Village Initiative.

One of our greatest gifts are the stories we have. In *Not Forgotten*, Wendi invites us along as she shares her journey of growing and raising a family through adoption. Wendi reminds us, in the most beautiful and honest way, how having the faith to say yes and to step into what the Lord is calling each of us into is one of the greatest stories we will ever get to tell. The story of Wendi and her son Neb invites us to experience God's goodness at its fullness. Joy, grief, struggle, peace, disappointment, and great celebration. All of it reminds us that our stories are never linear or how we think they should be, but when they are walked in surrender and belief in what we cannot yet understand or see, they will turn out to be better than we could have ever imagined or created on our own. Thank you, Wendi, for having the courage to say yes and share how God showed up in your story.

—**Pete Vargas,** CEO and Founder of Advance Your Reach.

Not Forgotten

WENDI CROSS

FUSION
HYBRID PUBLISHING

Library of Congress Control Number: 2024904390
Hardback ISBN: 9781637072205
Paperback ISBN: 9781637972212
eBook ISBN: 9781637972229

Cover by Dan Pitts
Interior Design by Typewriter Creative Co.

Printed in the United States of America
10 9 8 7 6 5 4 3 2 1

To my parents, whose love has been unconditional, my husband, who has covered me in prayer and protection, my incredible children, who are living for Jesus every day, and my grandchildren, who will someday read these words as proof of God's faithfulness. May each of you always pursue your own relationship with Jesus and be willing to say, "Yes, Lord, send me!"

CONTENTS

FOREWORD

by Nebeyu Cross

Growing up in Ethiopia, I experienced a lot of loss throughout my life. I lost my mom when I was two years old. I then went to live with my grandmother. She passed away only a couple, short years later.

As I grew up, I felt like God was taking everything I loved from me. Doubt set in, and I began to question God, "Why would you take everyone I love from me?"

I didn't know it at the time, but my heart became hard toward giving love to others and receiving love. I started to build up invisible, yet powerful walls, assuring people would not have access to my love. I started to believe all the lies the enemy told me.

You are not worthy of being loved.

If you love someone, they will die, because you are cursed.

No one sticks around.

If you get close to someone they will leave.

These thoughts went on for a very long time. They replayed over and over in my heart and mind. To make things worse, I lost my dad when I was twelve years old. At that point, all those prior lies I tried to deny became my truth.

Upon coming to America, I started to drift away from God. I watered those lies the enemy planted in me by rebelling against those who loved me. I became like a tree ready to fall at any moment. I blamed God for everything. I was angry at God for the loss I experienced. When I reached my teenage years, I started to understand what had happened to me. I counted the loss and grief, and I focused on it. I went on and on thinking about what was wrong with my life instead of what was right. I stopped believing in God.

I remember when I was fifteen driving home from soccer practice looking over at my adoptive mom right in her eyes and saying, "I don't think I'm even a Christian anymore."

I did so many things that I am not proud of. I was chasing after the world instead of what God had for me.

Thankfully, change started to happen for me in college. I began my college education majoring in construction management because that is the career of my adoptive dad. One day, as I was sitting in my English class, something just hit me. I suddenly felt like I was supposed to use my life struggles to help people who grew up in similar circumstances as I did.

After praying, I changed my major to social work. I was still working toward believing in God. My faith was not yet strong. My healing came when I returned to Ethiopia in 2017. I had forgotten what God had done for me because I was so focused on the wrong things. Instead of seeing God's steadfast love and faithfulness, I had chosen to see broken things. God started to work in me. The healing power of Jesus began to make me new again. All the lies I believed, all the walls I built, were being torn down by the love of God.

Day by day my faith grew, my hurts were healed, and I knew that I wanted my mom to help write my story. I was stuck for a bit, but God didn't leave me there. I truly hope this book can help people who are going through similar struggles of grief and loss. I hope it encourages the young people who are turning away from God. I pray it brings peace to parents praying for their children. I hope families read this book together and see how God is faithful even through the times we feel most alone. God is faithful!

And finally, to the families who are in the same place as my parents were, I pray you understand that it will take time for children from trauma to love you. Be patient, it doesn't happen overnight. With so much loss, confusion, fear, and struggles, these children are going through more than they can understand. I know it can be hard to not feel the love of the child you bring into your family through adoption, foster care, kinship, or marriage, but understand this, the child is trying.

Let me share from experience things that my parents did that truly helped me to heal and attach. They prayed for me always. They waited patiently for healing. They kept a gratitude journal of every good thing they saw in me and they said those things to me often. They tried to understand where I was coming from.

Now, let me tell where I felt most frustrated with my parents. They tried to force me to show them love in ways they expected. They couldn't relate to me. They didn't experience what I had experienced, but sometimes they would say they understood. They didn't understand. They wanted to, but they didn't. We all learned how to heal, how to love, and how to become a family.

Let my stories encourage you to keep showing up for one another. Show them you are there for them, waiting for them to receive your love, just as God is waiting for us to return to him.

Nebeyu Cross

INTRODUCTION

Dear Broken Heart,

I see you. I stand with you in this time of searching and listen to your sorrow as if your words are my own. When you feel alone and forgotten, I give you the time and space to process the seasons in your life. I hope through these pages you'll come to know from our stories that the promises of God always stand true. In the waiting, He hears you. In the loneliness, He is with you. In the broken, He is near. He's faithful in the unknown.

My heart is reflecting on the seven years of waiting for our son, Neb, to believe those promises. I didn't sit idle but spent seven years of waiting on God as I fought in prayer, consistently fasted, and wondered to myself if I possessed the faith even as small as a mustard seed. I mean, I thought I did, but the mountains remained unmoved.

Our twelve-year-old adopted son woke early to worship just as he had in the orphanage, making his bed and all his siblings' beds, just to feel accepted. He hid his emotions and acted strong. He lashed out at me as if I were his worst enemy, and he went through the motions.

However, his broken heart was not being mended. It remained in shambles, shattered as if shards of glass that seemed impossible to put back together. I refused to believe that for him and clung to the hope of healing to take place someday!

Our son came to us with a broken heart. He experienced the loss of both parents, and survived homelessness while living in cornfields. He experienced true hunger, betrayal, danger, and physical pain. He experienced loneliness, abandonment, rejection, and was forced into survival mode.

When Neb finally received placement in Covenant Orphanage at age eight, his circumstances changed for the better, but his heart didn't immediately mend. He desired to be joyful and live freely, but it felt impossible. He wanted to believe the unbelievable, that God loved him, but questioned that truth from the depth of his heartache.

The kids who bully you, the loneliness you feel eating alone at lunch, your parents' divorce, the sadness that creeps in whispering *you are not enough* is so painful. The expectations to be perfect, the pretend-to-be-funny personality you use to cover up insecurities, the broken promises of those who claim they love you, and the dark thoughts that haunt you as you close your eyes at night are all painful. If God's promises are always fulfilled, where is He now? Where is He in the pain and suffering?

I once believed healing came as soon as circumstances changed. As soon as we rescue the orphan, he or she receives healing. As soon as my parents repented and reconciled after the divorce, I would forgive them and move forward, unaffected. As soon as I moved to a new school, away from the mean kids, the slings and arrows of doubt would disappear. As soon as I stopped drinking alcohol, I would forgive myself for the many mistakes I made while drinking. I once believed when circumstances changed, healing quickly took place.

Now I know healing is a process, and it takes time. It is in the very character of God to provide us with this healing, but it doesn't happen immediately, and it is not easy. Rarely does healing happen miraculously. Healing almost always happens with a purpose and intention that we may not see in our time of brokenness.

During Nebeyu's pain, over time I realized God did make all things good for Neb. The pain was not erased, but God used what the enemy intended for harm and turned it for good. This means, while you are waiting for breakthrough and healing, you can turn to God who desires GOOD for you.

"And we know that God causes everything to work together for the good of those who love God and are called according to his purpose for them" (Romans 8:28).

For seven long years, Neb and I worked on our mother-son relationship. We made our time together memorable, full of laughter, fun, and adventure. We traveled for competitive soccer, and I became his biggest fan. We developed a spirit of gratitude for our beautifully messy, colorful family. We enjoyed one another and celebrated life together. However, under all the fun, part of Neb's heart remained behind walls I couldn't tear down. I spent countless nights on my knees pleading with God. I tried everything to connect deeply, but nothing seemed to work. Sometimes I felt the harder I tried, the more Neb retreated to be alone. I became so discouraged.

Neb no more understood how or why he walled himself off, or where the need to build the barriers even came from. Even so, he was ashamed and didn't understand why he couldn't feel more thankful and happy for everything he had at home with us.

We raised funds for a year, emptied our savings, traveled across the world, and adopted him into our family. God used us to answer his most urgent and consistent prayer for a family. Even Neb felt bad he couldn't attach to and show us affection the way we anticipated he'd love us. We prayed for God to heal the wounds.

Do you have a hard time believing in love? Do you believe God can heal your broken and discouraged heart? We can dig deep and tear down walls, but it takes purpose and work. Even when we don't believe it, God sees it and He can give us the power to overcome. I didn't know that after we adopted Nebeyu we would need to seek outside counseling. I thought counseling was for people who were weak and didn't know Jesus. This is simply untrue. Anything requiring change takes effort and perseverance. Change also takes time. I expected immediate results.

Healing Takes Work

Our family learned patience and perseverance and built a lot of character along the way. It took years of praying, fasting, studying God's word, talking to professionals, worshipping together, and managing lots of conflicts be-fore we could start deep and transparent conversations. This vulnerability eventually led to Neb's freedom. He had hardened his heart solely on lies the enemy whispered— lies such as: *You didn't even cry when your mom died. You can't just get a new mom when you didn't even grieve your first mom.*

Neb was less than two years old and nursing when his biological mother passed. Even though he was a baby, he expected himself to properly grieve her death. It seems obviously unrealistic to us that a two-year-old little boy can know how to process that kind of grief. However, Neb believed this lie as truth, and it was his reality.

Love and perseverance were the antidote to healing.

I often wondered how long it would take to see healing in my son's life. The trauma he experienced caused me to ponder how God would work His miracle. I waited. We worked hard. We took a few steps forward and then, with-out warning, the arguing and fighting returned. I didn't give up on Neb because I knew God didn't give up on me. In the waiting, I wrestled, and I prayed just like the father of the child in the Bible called out, "Please, God, help me with my unbelief."

Wherever you are on your journey, be encouraged. You can have unbelief and still be near to God. You can take the time you need to grieve.

You must be willing to dig deep. Counseling is not for the weak, but for the brave.

It takes work to heal a broken heart, but like Neb, I am believing and trusting the process for you. I pray as you read our family's adoption story, you will feel Neb's pain and see God as He walks Neb through the healing process. Many of you will relate to the feelings of abandonment, loss, betrayal, abuse, and hopelessness. Although Neb may not have always felt God's presence, we are confident God was, and is, always nearby!

He is also near to you.

Right now, He is near. As you read the pages ahead, know God is knocking. There is healing available, and you can be set free. Your broken heart can be mended. There is hope for you. God can use your story to encourage others.

Nothing you are going through is wasted. In fact, you can stand on the same promise we stood. God will never leave you nor forsake you. He will work all things together for the good of those who love Him. You may feel lonely, but you are not alone. Our family is living proof of God's promises.

I'd like to invite you now to turn the page, meet my family, and imagine yourself sitting next to me on my front porch, sipping on a cool glass of freshly squeezed lemonade. Get to know us; let's become friends!

Fear no evil!

1

FATHERLESSNESS

"God is everything a perfect father should be.
He is our protector, provider, healer, creator,
sustainer, corrector, and comforter."[1]

The phone rang. When I heard my husband's voice on the other end, I knew my life was about to change. He called me from an internet café in Ethiopia. My 6'6", 330-pound rock of a man fought back tears.

His voice cracked. I heard his brokenness. I felt his heartbreak. This broad-shouldered, solid-to-the-core man sat in an internet café halfway around the world with tears falling like rain on a keyboard. Nobody there in Ethiopia would have missed this larger-than-life man with pale skin leaning over a laptop, tears streaming down his face. The year was 2008. All our lives were about to change drastically. I knew it. And I admit, I was nervous, even fearful. Frantically, I prayed.

---

1   Family, ORBC. "Our Heavenly Father Vs. Our Earthly Fathers." Oak Ridge Baptist Church. Last modified April 24, 2020. https://www.orbcfamily.org/blog/faith/our-heavenly-father-vs-our-earthly-fathers/.

Lord, please prepare my heart because I am not ready to serve in Africa or give more than we are already giving.

True Orphan (2003)

Five-year-old Neb waited for his dad to return home from work. Mohammed was a security guard and traveled all over the country to find work. Some jobs kept him away from the family for weeks at a time, and employment opportunities closer to the village made it possible for him to return home late in the evenings. Mohammad was an absent father, mostly, and often found at local bars drinking and smoking. He left the caretaking of the children to his many wives.

When Neb's biological mother passed away, one of his stepmothers moved into the house. When Mohammed was in town, she tolerated Neb and his older sister, Kedija. However, as soon as Mohammed left town, she turned abusive toward the children. She saw Neb and Kedija as a burden and despised the space they occupied and the food they ate. Left with little option, this forced them to survive outside on their own. Hiding in the cornfields at night to sleep, Kedija and Neb huddled together to stay warm, but also to stay safe. The dirt roads of Holeta, Ethiopia, were no place for two children running around alone. The dangers for a thirteen-year-old little girl were unfathomable. Every day, Kedija was at risk of being raped and taken as a sex slave.

Instead of being fearful of her future, Kedija took on the mother role for young Neb. They walked the streets during the day, scavenging for food. Thankfully, many of their biological mom's friends worked in the market selling fruits and vegetables. Those ladies promised her on her deathbed to keep Neb and Kedija safe. They pinched and scraped to provide at least one small snack a day, but they too struggled with poverty.

After about three years of this unstable family life, Neb's father became critically ill. Having done all they could do for him, the doctors gave little hope of survival.

Desperate to look out for her brother, Kedija took it upon herself, now sixteen years old, to apply for Neb to be accepted into a new orphanage opening in Holeta.

Covenant Orphanage was only open for children who had lost both mother and father, "true orphans," but with Kedija's determination to change the course of her little brother's life, this only made her more resolute. Mere survival was not enough. She wanted more for him. He deserved to be loved and safe in a happy, healthy home. Kedija knew the sacrifice as she completed the application for Neb. In her heart, she understood an American family might adopt him and take him far away. She anguished over the thought of never seeing him again, but she knew the decision was the right one.

Kedija also understood, for her to survive, she needed to make another difficult decision. She signed a contract to be a servant in Dubai.

Days before their father passed, Kedija traveled to see him, papers in hand. She prayed along the way, hoping to convince him to sign the request for placement. She feared his refusal, but her love for Neb outweighed her fear.

She held onto hope, but Covenant Orphanage was

a Christian children's home, and Mohammed was a Muslim. Her request would likely meet resistance.

Nervously, Kedija approached her dying father. She told the truth about their stepmother and her treatment of her and Neb in Mohammad's absence. She shared about her decision to leave for work in Dubai. She insisted he make it possible for Neb to have hope for a future. Taking a deep breath, she waited for his answer.

After a long, thoughtful pause, Mohammed voiced no reservations and signed the paperwork. Each obstacle disappeared, and against the odds, Covenant Orphanage accepted Neb. He received a bed, clothes, shoes, food, and love—all the things missing since his mother's passing six years earlier. It felt like a miracle. Kedija, much too young to make such sacrificial, weighty decisions, managed like a hero.

Two short weeks after moving into the orphanage, Neb learned Mohammed passed away. He then became a "true orphan," left to grieve the loss of his last living parent, alone and surrounded by strangers.

Grateful While Grieving (2004)

I know the pain and grief of losing a father, but in losing my father, I experienced a very different loss.

I was pregnant with our third son, Cooper. A few weeks before my due date, I received a phone call from my dad that I'll never forget. From the trembling of his voice, I knew instantly something was terribly wrong.

"I'm going to prison."

I never dreamed my father would ever utter such words.

He assured me of his innocence and that he planned to fight the accusations. Although he tried his best to comfort me that he would be all right, the uncertainty I heard in his tear-filled voice left me feeling anything but assurance.

How could something like this could happen to my dad? *My* dad? My *daddy?*

The dad who coached all my soccer teams when I was a little girl. The dad who took me to doctor appointments and bribed me with new shoes after immunizations. The dad who welcomed in my cousins when their parents couldn't take care of them. The dad who taught me to give my meals to the man on the corner holding a sign. The dad I idolized my entire life. What could possibly have happened to put him in this mess? My mind raced and my thoughts spun in circles. The questions. The disbelief. The fear. The anger! Oh, the anger at such accusations. And the knot in my stomach. I wanted to vomit.

After more than a year of investigations, my dad lost everything.

This forced him to sell our twenty-five-acre ranch to pay attorney fees. The storyline of accusations was simply untrue, and our family knew it. We clung to hope. Surely the jury would see the truth, too. Surely. Innocent until proven guilty, right? There was no way to prove his guilt in a crime he didn't commit, right? We prayed and hoped and trusted justice would win.

The trial lasted two long and grueling months. Then the verdict came. The prosecution created a false timeline, but unfortunately, the jury believed it.

Guilty. Life in prison.

When I learned of the verdict, I crumpled to the floor in my office six hundred miles away, curled up in the fetal position, and wailed as if he had died. I wailed and cried, and wailed and cried some more. I shed more tears than I thought possible, and I became paralyzed with anger. I learned what it meant to lament.

It was 2004. He was alive, but his life was gone. Mine changed forever. His grandchildren's lives changed forever. The lives of everyone who ever knew or loved him changed.

Burning anger swallowed me. Grief overwhelmed me and dropped me to my knees. What does one do with all that emotion? I questioned God.

How could God know the truth, see the truth, hear our prayers, and then let the story end like this? For what purpose is my dad spending life in prison for something he didn't do? Why didn't they see his innocence? What do I do with this feeling of helplessness?

Dad continues to work on an appeal to this day.

He refused to take the plea bargain, which would have allowed him to be released in 2011, seven years served. Taking that plea meant admitting to something he didn't do. He refused.

As I enter the prison gates on my visits, I still question the purpose of this loss. My dad can't go to his grandkids. He has spent over seventeen years in prison, still with no foreseeable way out. I wonder in the waiting: God, will justice ever be served here on earth for my dad and my family? When can I have my daddy back? Will he die in prison?

True, my dad didn't die. I still see him during visits. I can hear his voice on the other end of the phone. I get to be his pen pal, but he has lost life. And I've lost much of what would have been.

Over time, God has taught me to grieve the loss of time we could have spent together and still be grateful he is still with us. Losing a parent can be from something more than death—divorce, abandonment, addictions, betrayal, and more.

In death, I know it is more difficult to remain hopeful on this side of heaven, such as with Neb. He will never see, touch, hear, or even have the opportunity to write letters to his biological mom or dad. Loss hurts.

Our earthly fathers, whether dead or alive, cannot and will not ever be a perfect description of our Heavenly Father. Earthly fathers fall short. Even the best fathers in the world mess up. Mommies fall short too, almost daily. I say and do things I shouldn't, and sometimes don't do things I should. That's just more proof we all need Jesus!

Many see the lives of Christians and call our sin issues hypocrisy. However, according to God's Word, our mistakes are the reason we need Jesus. We need forgiveness. We need redemption. We need second, third, fourth chances, or more. We need the blood that washes away sin and forgiveness, and so do our parents. This is why He died on the cross.

Friend, I hope you realize we don't see ourselves as better, perfect, or good. We see ourselves as flawed and weak. It is in our weakness and in our flaws that we find the strength, forgiveness, and redemption of Jesus Christ through our belief, faith, and in our lives surrendered to Him.

Believing His death and resurrection in faith is all we need to claim His promises. If you have yet to put your hope and faith in Jesus, I pray the words you've read and those on the pages ahead are enough to lead you to the Cross. If you are ready now, I have included my personal testimony and an example prayer at the back of the book.

2

CHILDREN ARE A
GIFT FROM GOD

*"Children are a gift from the Lord; they are a reward
from him. Children born to a young man are like
arrows in a warrior's hands. How joyful is the man
whose quiver is full of them!"* (Psalm 127:3-5).

Within our first five years of marriage, I was pregnant
three times. Our family expanded to four with two boys,
five-year-old Colby and one-year-old Casey, with the loss
of a baby between the two.

Before our third child entered the world, I settled into a
comfortable rhythm of motherhood. Having two children
didn't seem so difficult. I took everything in stride.

Rick knew my heart and understood my desire for a
daughter, so he convinced me we should try at least one
more time. It's hard to admit now, but I prepared for my
ultrasound sporting all the pink power I could possess. I
arrived wearing all pink, all the way down to pink pant-
ies—as if pink wielded any kind of actual power.

Silly, I know. It's not as if I thought any of my efforts

determined anything, or as if another boy wouldn't fill me with great joy. I just deeply hoped for a girl, and tried hard to will it so, even knowing we would celebrate whoever God gave us.

I held my breath, in my mind at least, and listened to the rhythmic whooshing of the baby's heartbeat. I watched in anticipation as the doctor rolled the scanning device over my abdomen. And there it was.

"Well, you can see that thing from across the room," the doctor pronounced as he pointed at specifics on the monitor.

I knew it. Another boy. I fought back the tears, willing them not to fall, because I knew the truth. *Every* child is a gift from God, including another boy. However, I hate to admit, I sulked a bit. I just kept wondering if I would ever have a baby girl. I've heard it said that boys often move away when they're adults, and girls stay close to home. Even then, I wondered if all my kids would grow up and leave me because they were boys.

At least my pregnancy with Cooper was a breeze compared to the other three.

Colby

As a collegiate cheerleader on scholarship, I took good care of my body. I was in the best shape of my life when I became pregnant with Colby, our first-born son. The demands of a cheerleader athlete kept me super active. Pairing that with the important emphasis I placed on my nutrition, I weighed a whole one-hundred fifteen pounds soaking wet. My abs, a solid six-pack and more muscle than fat back then, are not so solid now. Oh, how fun it was to be young when eating a donut and working out for three hours was the norm.

By the time our due date arrived, I was all done. When I say, "all done," I mean I tried everything to go into labor. I even talked my husband's best friend into taking me four-wheeling in hopes the bumpy ride would break my water. I walked around a high school track over eight miles without stopping for water once. I stretched, took a bath, and walked some more. In fact, I ambled so much, my ankles swelled to the size of a baby elephant. I thought I was doing a good thing, until I arrived at my check-up and learned otherwise.

My doctor gave me that look. You know, the concerned, questioning, maybe-a-little-annoyed-you've-overdone-it look. Yep. That one. Then he spoke.

"Wendi Cross, what have you been doing today? Your heart is racing, your blood pressure is high, and you have toxemia. You will be heading straight to the hospital from here to be induced." And that was that.

Well, that is one way to go into labor. I guess all my hard work paid off. It's probably a good thing I only thought it, because I doubt my doctor would have found it amusing.

We called Rick away from football practice. He was in his junior year playing defensive tackle at The University of Nevada, Reno. He borrowed a truck from one of his coaches to meet me at the hospital. I wanted labor, and I got it. Once induced, I tried breathing throughout the contractions just as we learned in our birthing class, but as each minute passed and each contraction intensified, my initial desire for an all-natural birth quickly switched to wanting all the meds.

"Give me everything and give it to me now!" I didn't ask. I'm reasonably sure I didn't use my best inside voice, either.

When the anesthesiologist administered the epidural, it gave me immediate relief. I took a nap while my body prepared itself for childbirth. After twenty hours of labor, Colby entered the world on his due date, April 21, 1998. A healthy baby boy, weighing seven pounds seven ounces. I held this perfect gift from God and finally understood unconditional love. He was perfectly and wonderfully made. I was a mom.

After exactly six weeks of recovery, I put my cheer uniform back on, began training, regained my scholarship, and returned to the sidelines to cheer for my husband and the Nevada Wolf Pack team. To pick up right where I had left off felt like a dream come true.

Casey

I developed gestational diabetes with Casey, was restricted to bedrest, and given a strict diet. Ugh. That was awful. Let's just say I wasn't always successful. In fact, slightly rebellious describes it better. I found it nearly impossible to deny the cravings for Fruity Pebbles, Cocoa Pebbles, and all kinds of other yummy carb-filled, sugary things. I soon learned if I waited until the middle of the night, after dinner but before morning, I could eat a whole bowl of Fruity Pebbles and still pass my blood poke early the next morning. When my cravings got the best of me, I waited until Colby and Rick were fast asleep, then I slipped from the bed and tiptoed into the kitchen, conscious of every movement to avoid making the slightest noise. Did the calories really count if I only cheated in the middle of the night when nobody was looking?

I carried Casey to full-term, and his birth weight was six pounds thirteen ounces my smallest baby, so I feel like I did well. I surely could've eaten more Fruity Pebbles and still been fine. I tried to follow the food plan, but pregnancy is way more fun when we give ourselves permission to enjoy all those temporary cravings, right?

Even delivery with Cooper differed from the others.

Cooper (aka Coop)

Our morning started out like every other normal school day, including carpool duty with my white minivan full of kids. I dropped off Colby and his kindergarten friends around 8 a.m. Shortly thereafter, the first labor pains hit. Having been through birth twice before, I knew the process and the waiting involved. So, like a real veteran, I talked myself into enduring the pain throughout the day. After all, I fully planned to fulfill my carpool duty, and at 3:30 p.m. I needed to pick up not only my two children, but three others from two different families.

The contractions continued throughout the day, increasing in intensity, but still manageable. Afternoon came, and I returned to school to fill the minivan with kids once again.

Big and pregnant, walking through the halls holding my side, raised a few eyebrows. When I saw the questions on their faces, I confirmed their concerns by telling them I was indeed in labor. They surely probed my sanity. I admit. It was probably crazy. But to my thinking, I still had so much to do, and too many arrangements needed to be made before I left for the hospital that night. While driving home, I kept running the lengthy to-do list through my mind, making mental notes of all the unchecked boxes. We lived in Las Vegas without family nearby, so I needed to figure out dinner for my kids. I kept thinking it was such a burden to have one of Rick's coworkers come over and stay all night.

As I dropped off the carpool kids, I stopped to pick up pizzas. Dinner, check. I hardly knew Rick's coworker and didn't want to burden her more than necessary. I knew I was pushing it, no pun intended, but I was in full mommy mode. Definitely nesting.

After all of that, I called Rick. He needed to meet me at home and take me to the hospital. It was time. He walked in, without a hint of excitability, and looked at me. To him, I appeared to be doing just fine.

"Do I have time for a quick shower?"

Poor guy. He asked the wrong question of a woman having been in all-day labor. I kind of lost my mind and flung back an adamant response.

"Absolutely not. Get in the car!"

We arrived at the hospital a few minutes later and headed straight for the elevator. Rick selected the appropriate floor, and we began our ascent. I soon realized I had progressed into full labor, an almost-ready-to-push kind of labor, and the contractions came only seconds apart.

Without a doubt, I was ready for an epidural. It seemed like an eternity before the elevator came to a stop, and a sweet nurse greeted me when the doors opened. Between the labor pains and breathing, I told her I was there to have my baby. She looked stunned. She patiently guided me to the nurse's station to fill out paperwork.

What? Paperwork? At a time like this? Ugh!

As the contractions increased, my frustrations also grew. "This is my third child. I've been in labor all day, and I am ready for an epidural right now!" I still can't believe I spewed like that to that poor, unsuspecting nurse.

But there I stood, hunkered over in pain, not even yet checked in, and dying for an epidural. I needed that hospital bracelet because I needed the epidural waiting for me. I needed it right then, as if they would give it to me standing at the nurses' station as soon as they slapped that bracelet on me.

Being the professional she was, the nurse calmly explained the anesthesiologist was heading into surgery and it would be at least two hours before he could get to me.

"No! He must do my epidural before he goes into surgery or it will be too late," I said, gritting my teeth.

"It doesn't usually work that way," she said, "but I will ask him." For some reason, she listened to me. I didn't understand it, but I was grateful.

With the sign-in process completed, they found a hospital bed for me and immediately began checking me over. Sure enough, I was dilated to seven and ready for that epidural, just as I insisted. I mean, a woman knows, right? Especially one who's taken this trip a time or two before.

Just over an hour later, I was ready to push. Thanks to the amazing epidural, delivery seemed so uneventful. I pushed for only a few minutes before I heard his cries. Seriously, I watched the season finale of *The Bachelor* while the medical team applied stitches.

Don't judge. Reality TV is my weakness.

Game Over

We quickly learned Coop was a force to be reckoned with. Our third little blessing gave us a run for our money. When it was just Colby and Casey, life still seemed more doable. God gave them both easy temperaments. They were sociable, patient, and adaptable. Coop, on the other hand, clearly knew his role as the little brother of the three. He was born with a fighting spirit.

What Coop wanted, Coop was going to get. And even more challenging, what Coop didn't want to do, Coop didn't do.

Even at just two days old, clicking him into his car seat prompted hysteria. How did he even know he didn't like being in the car? And how could such a tiny package produce such an ear-piercing, deafening scream? Even the kids in my carpool opted out of riding with us to school. What were we to do but endure? We had to go places. We couldn't stay home simply because "Super Cooper" didn't like the car.

Once, my best friend Erin and I drove the kids from Las Vegas to Reno to meet our families and celebrate the new baby. I warned Erin about Coop and car rides, but she shrugged it off. She agreed to drive so I could cater to his demands. After all, he was only two weeks old. Erin was convinced he would eventually cry himself to sleep. I thought so, too.

Five minutes into the trip, the blood-curdling screams began. I tried everything. We stopped multiple times to change diapers and to nurse, but the second I buckled him back in that car seat, the screaming started all over again. I am certain our kids held their hands over their ears for a nonstop six hours. Throughout the entire drive, Coop never slept. All the way to Reno he cried. I cried. We all cried. By the time he turned two years old, I was exhausted. I looked at my husband and told him I didn't need a daughter after all. I truly believed this was game over. The boys won. We were done.

Even our license plate read: GAME OVER: BOYS 3, GIRLS 0.

Little Sister

The three boys kept us busy for the next few years. Life resembled organized chaos: hectic, loud, and fun. I began to believe I was created to be a Boy Mom. Even my dad once said, "Wendi, God wants you to raise up some godly husbands and fathers." I took his instruction and encouragement to heart. If God created me to raise godly husbands and fathers, then I would do that to the best of my ability.

I surrendered and settled into my Boy Mom role, but then something changed. When Coop was about three years old, Rick made a confession. He had been praying with some persistency that my unanswered prayer for a daughter would be answered. He wanted one more child.

I waited and prayed. I tried to reconcile another child might give us another boy, almost enough for our own basketball team. I needed to know if we had another son, we would not feel disappointed.

Before long, we learned we were expecting. Rick was confident we were having a daughter. As it turned out, he was right. We were ecstatic to learn we were having a girl! I will never forget that ultrasound. As the monitor went over my abdomen, our doctor paused and smiled. He knew our prayers. He took a screenshot of her and said, "Prayers answered."

Cami Angelica Cross was born to be a little sister. She takes her role seriously and her big brothers dote over her. The boys loved helping with her, and she adored every minute. Sometimes, the boys had to be removed from her room and away from her crib. They always offered some excuse about hearing her wake up and went in there to keep her happy. Cami brought an abundance of joy our way. I dressed her like a baby doll with tutus and bows. Big ones, because I like big bows—the bigger, the better. Our home felt full.

We needed to update our license plate to our new final score: BOYS 3: GIRLS 1.

Or so we thought.

I'm a bit thick in the skull, but I learned the game is never really over as long as we still breathe. God's ways are not our ways, and His thoughts are higher than our thoughts. God was far from finished growing our family.

The game was far from over, and we had no idea.

3

COMING HOME PART I

*"Now faith is confidence in what we hope for and
assurance about what we do not see"* (Hebrews 11:1).

Deep Faith

Rick played college football with a friend committed to
mission work in Ethiopia. We believed in John and his
wife and their mission, so we supported the ministry financially. Their faith inspired us. We witnessed their
adoption story firsthand as they opened their home and
welcomed an orphaned child.

Our involvement stopped there until one day when
John invited Rick to go with him on their next mission
trip. After an alumni football game in Reno, Rick and I
joined John and his wife, Terina, for a walk, enjoying each
other's company and catching up on life. We listened to
John and Terina share their stories of the life-changing work of their mission for the children at Covenant
Orphanage. Their stories and their passion intrigued us
both. However, traveling to Africa seemed like the most

WENDI CROSS

farfetched idea, at least one nobody had ever thrown our way. We had recently moved back to California, and Rick had started a new job in construction management. Leaving for a two-week trip to Africa seemed unrealistic. Why would his boss ever approve of his absence for so long, and so soon? No way.

Undeterred, but patient, John continued to pursue Rick about joining him on the trip. My husband kept shrugging it off until John's final invitation appealed to my husband's left-brain thinking. Rick wasn't ready for a blind leap of faith, so John tried logic.

"Rick, why don't you come and see where and how your money is being used?"

John's question struck a chord.

"I'll ask for the time off, and IF my boss agrees, I will join you."

Being a man of his word, Rick approached his boss at his next opportunity. I'm confident he felt sure he'd hear a quick, punctuated "No." End of story.

But God had other ideas.

"That sounds like an incredible opportunity. I think you should go."

His boss didn't even hesitate. In less than two weeks, Rick was on a flight to Uganda and Ethiopia, a trip that forever changed his life and ours.

A Call from a Cafe

I expected Rick to call once they got settled. After all, neither of us had ever been to Africa, and he took this adventure without me. I stayed home with the children, ages eleven, six, four, and one. My heart leaped when I heard the familiar ringtone.

Just a few words into the conversation, I heard his voice crack. My 6'6", 330-pound rock was fighting back tears. I heard his brokenness. I felt his heartbreak. In that moment, I knew my life would never be the same. This brings us back to that internet café call. The one where my broad-shouldered husband had broken down into tears streaming down his face. I knew all our lives were about to change drastically. I admit, my nerves caused quakes within me. I felt fearful. Frantically, I prayed.

Lord, please prepare my heart because I am not ready to serve in Africa or give more than we are already giving.

When Rick returned from Ethiopia, he wasted no time inviting over those closest to us. He couldn't wait to share his experience and to cast a vision. He worked with a sense of urgency, selling things and asking others to join us. He was determined to make a difference, one child at a time. On fire to birth a non-profit, he pressed on with purpose every single day. He gathered. He shared. He gave. He worked. He planned.

The vision caught flame and our non-profit, xHope, was born.

While we were hard at work sharing stories about the children Rick had met, Neb was living at Covenant Orphanage in Ethiopia losing hope he would ever have a family. He clung to the fatherlike mentorship John, Rick, and the guys would give while on site. However, that was temporary. Each time these guys came and went, Neb grasped every minute of time he could with them. Neb wore a gray athletic pantsuit which was three inches too short, not because he didn't have clothes that fit, but because that athletic suit was a Christmas gift from John years earlier in 2006.

Neb deeply valued the gifts, but the words of encouragement and quality time the men shared with Neb and the other children were equally important. When the men returned to the states, Neb's life at the orphanage consisted of being a shepherd boy herding sheep and goats. He rose early to care for them, take them out to pasture, watch over them, and corral them back into the gates of Covenant as the sun set.

Perfect Timing

Neb waited and prayed for a family for nearly four years. He watched the children's home fill up and empty more than once. A young child or baby stood a better chance of being adopted sooner. Older children typically waited longer and risked never finding a forever family. In Ethiopia, when a child turned thirteen, adoption was no longer an option.

When Neb turned eleven, the window of hope seemed to be closing. Time was running out.

Although Neb feared he might lose the opportunity to be adopted because of his age, he continued to pray and hope for a forever family. The good news is, Neb prayed to a living God who is always right on time.

God does things in His time, for His purpose, and for His glory. And God executes with His perfect timing.

Mothers of Sons

After Rick returned from Ethiopia, he brought more than a fire with him. He returned with a photo album filled with pictures of each child awaiting adoption at Covenant Orphanage. A short bio description accompanied each child's photo. We read through the album and prayed nightly for the children at Covenant. Rick and I felt committed to prayer as one way to advocate for these waiting children. We memorized their names and prayed for their forever families. After each "Amen," nights grew more and more sleepless.

One night after looking through the album, I laid there staring at the ceiling for hours, unable to fall asleep to the familiar cadence of my husband's snoring. This night my restlessness felt different. My spirit was unsettled, and I kept replaying a quote I had heard.

"If you can do it, why are you praying for someone else to?"

As I turned toward the fireplace, I fixed my eyes on a picture frame of myself and my three sons. It was lit up like a pot of gold. The frame read, "Mothers of sons believe in who they will become."

Somehow, in that moment, I envisioned the image of the oldest boy in the orphanage in that frame alongside my boys. The clock ticked fast for eleven-year-old Neb. Time was running out for him to be adopted. My oldest son was Neb's same age. My heart broke. I swallowed hard and closed my eyes fighting back the tears. I couldn't help thinking, *What if something ever happened to*

Rick and me and nobody would take Colby because he was an older boy?

I sucked in a gasp. It was the aha moment of all aha moments.

I don't know about you, but sometimes God's messages hit me like a ton of bricks—and a little too often, if I'm honest. In that moment, I felt the weight of the whole load.

With frantic enthusiasm, and a serious lack of anything gentle, I shook the snoring bear next to me. Startled, Rick sat up ready to tackle a home invader, but melted immediately when he saw my tears. I prayed for God to give me a heart for the children, just as He had given to Rick. God answered that prayer.

"Rick, I think we should adopt Neb."

"Oh my gosh, Wend, I know you have your hands full with the four kiddos. I wouldn't have ever asked you to adopt, but if you are willing, please start the paperwork tomorrow."

That was that. No hesitation. We took the leap.

With very little knowledge of international adoption, I awoke early and dove hard into the research. I called our missionary friends to share our plans. We asked them to pray with us and to keep it quiet until we were far enough along in the process to share the news with friends and family. As new Christians, barely learning to walk in our budding relationship with Christ, this leap of faith was huge. To us, this felt like something one reads about in the lives of others. Soon, words from the song

"Oceans"[1] echoed in our lives. God was taking us deeper than our feet could ever wander, and our faith was being made so much stronger.

Blind faith. That's the best way to describe our decision. Believing without seeing. I firmly trust that God only gives us what we can handle for each day. He reminds us in His word that His grace is sufficient for today. We learned rather quickly to lean into this promise and stand firm regardless of how others responded. This was taking us deeper and deeper into the unknown. Loneliness sometimes set in, but the reward of a full house reminded us it would all be worth it.

We must press on! We knew Neb was to be our son, and we were determined to do everything possible to make it official.

The Adoption Process

The adoption process is not for the faint of heart. It's a never-giving-up kind of faith. We waited. We laughed. We cried. We waited some more. The final stages of simply waiting for approval felt like an eternity. We wondered if it would ever happen. Then it did.

The day our approval came, we were overjoyed. It felt like the labor pains of childbirth had just subsided, and the joy of all the hard work finally arrived. That approval was the answer to Neb's years of praying and our year of persistence. We felt the excitement of a gender reveal

---

1   Hillsong UNITED. "Oceans (Where Feet May Fail)." 4. Zion. Capitol CMG. 2013.

party when everyone shouts, "We're having a boy!" Then, wondering if the blessed event is a true moment, *Is it real?* The moment our dream became a reality, our prayer answered, and our family officially grew from four children to five, we held one another tight. We prayed a prayer of thanksgiving. We looked each other in the eyes and let the tears fall.

As soon as we received approval for the adoption, we sent Neb a picture book of our family.

When eleven-year-old Neb finally received the gift of a "family photo album," he became obsessed with it. The album, full of the "game-over crew" introducing themselves as his mom, dad, brothers, and little sister, symbolized hope to Neb. His forever family. His. And this photo album belonged to him, to cling to as he awaited his new family's arrival.

During the wait, Neb fed his hope by carrying the picture book everywhere he went. He showed everyone who visited. He memorized every page. He learned every name and birth date. He endeavored to read the words in English and practiced that vocabulary daily. Each day he waited for our arrival gave him one more day to practice.

Each day Neb waited, we also waited.

We knew early this true faith journey might cause concern and fear in those closest to us. God gave us wisdom to hold the announcement of our decision until everything was in motion. Our discernment can only be attributed to God because the opposition that came our way was nothing we expected. Had we asked for advice, there is a real possibility we might have been talked out of our decision to adopt. We didn't know then how many friends we would lose, the number of blatant rejections we would receive, the way we would experience racism for the first time, or how we would become outcasts to the people we once considered close to us. There was A LOT we didn't know then.

And God did what God does. He went before us.

Contrary to the negative responses, we also received overwhelming support from unexpected sources and from families we did not expect would support the adoption. This encouragement and support meant everything to us. We clung to those who prayed, supported, and encouraged us. Soccer families donated financially; people sold items just so they could contribute, including a car, and the proceeds were given toward our adoption. We watched God move the hearts of people and stood amazed to receive support from so many unexpected sources. And we experienced deep hurt by those we assumed would support us.

Before we ever asked for a dollar from others in our fundraising efforts, we emptied our savings of $8,000, applied for several adoption grants, and took a one-year break from all competitive sports and extracurricular activities, which required monthly fees. We made a decision as a family to sacrifice all we could to make this adoption process possible. In that year, we experienced more love and generosity than we could have ever imagined. Thinking back, my eyes still fill with tears, and my heart explodes with gratitude. When God says "go," He makes a way.

The most shocking gift came two days before we left for

Ethiopia. My husband's employers, small business owners, wowed us with their support and generosity by giving us a lump sum right before our travel. That generous donation not only provided the balance due to our adoption agency, but it was enough to purchase another plane ticket so our oldest son, Colby, could join us on the trip.

God knew Colby needed to be there, but at the time, we didn't realize the significance.

4

COMING HOME PART II

*"And do not forget to do good and to share with others,
for such sacrifices God is pleased."* (Hebrews 13:16).

Chosen

My husband's employers, Jeff and Margaret Reed, had no
idea the impact of the generous financial gift they gave us
before we traveled. God knew what was ahead, and He
provided. God knew Colby needed to be on that trip, and
God made it possible. He made a way. He provided.

The anticipation of meeting our son gave us all a roll-
er-coaster of feelings. Anxiety, excitement, anticipation,
joy, and gratitude. The fears of not raising enough money,
the what-if questions we asked.

"What if he doesn't like it here? What if he is rebellious? What if we can't love him as much as our biological
children? What if he is aggressive? What if..." had been
erased out of our hearts and minds like a marker on a
whiteboard. We were ready for this day. We were prepared. We needed to embrace our son.

On the other side of the world, Neb was feeling similar anticipation. He had waited for his forever family for years. He had prayed for us before he knew us. He had no fear about coming to America, having a new family, or living in a new culture. It is by the grace of God that Neb was finally getting what he had always asked God for, a mom, dad, and siblings. He waited and waited for us, and now we were coming for him.

When we walked through the gates of Covenant Orphanage, there was unspeakable joy. The kind of joy that is contagious. It was not just Neb and our family overflowing with laughter, hugs, and smiles, it was every waiting child who lived at Covenant Orphanage and every staff member. From the guard at the gate to the house mama, the welcome we experienced felt as though we were celebrities. Far from celebrities though, we were humbly walking in obedience to what God has laid on our hearts.

As our van pulled into the small, dirt driveway, the guard greeted us with a smile that covered his face, from ear to ear, every tooth showing. He waved his hands above his head as to enthusiastically celebrate our arrival. As he slowly opened the blue tin gate, we were greeted with the smiles and cheers of every child and staff member from Covenant Orphanage. As the children were waving us in and running alongside the van, our eyes filled with tears. All the nerves and anticipation had led us to this place.

As we exited the vehicle, Neb met us with a warm embrace. Me first. He wrapped his arms around my neck, he squeezed very tightly, and he said with perfect English, "Hi, Mom."

My knees went weak. I looked at his dark brown eyes, and I replied, "I love you, Son." I believe the love shared in that moment is the love we will share tangibly when we meet Jesus face-to-face and He embraces us. This display of love continued as Neb hugged Rick and Colby next. Colby knew upon meeting Neb that he had just met his forever best friend and older brother. It was an immediate connection where anticipation and reality collided. Like the ending of a fireworks show, our family had just experienced a supernatural, grand finale of unconditional love exploding.

I was greeted once again as Neb came back for seconds. He gave me a sweet hug, an additional kiss on the cheek, and in perfect English again said "Hi, Mom." He wanted to me to know he had practiced his English and knew my name. I was embraced by my newest and oldest son, older than Colby by six months. Everything we worked for over the last year, the sacrifices made, money spent, countless hours of prayer, loss of friends, courts, agencies, adoption classes, and the adoption journey, was all worth it. Neb embraced Colby next. Smiling he said, "Colby, my brother." Then he went to Rick, wrapped his arms around him, and held on tight for a long moment as Rick returned his embrace. In that moment, I felt Neb's joy overflowing. His dad came back for him. Neb took it all in. He felt chosen, at last. Rick chose Neb to be his son, giving him a forever family. God proved faithful to Neb yet again.

What a beautiful picture of how I believe we respond when we receive God's love for the first time. I imagine it being a long, freeing embrace of acceptance. He chooses us, and we get to rest in His protective arms. We get to know we have a Father who would go from Heaven to Earth just for us, just as Rick had gone from the United States to Ethiopia, just for Neb.

Fourth of July

After Neb's adoption, our family seemed complete, or so we thought. God knew better. We were clueless that our family would expand once again.

I was in the middle of cooking dinner when my phone rang. It had been almost a year since Neb had been home from Ethiopia. He was adjusting, we were adjusting, and our lives felt full. The chaos of cooking for five kids, homework sprawled out on the countertop for the middle boys, the view of my two big kids juggling the soccer ball on the back patio, and Cami playing with her pretend kitchen, made me feel like taking a call could create a true disaster. However, I felt prompted to answer because the caller ID said, "Sutter Medical Center."

My estranged cousin struggled deeply with a difficult life. Fifteen years had passed since the last time we saw each other. Then she called to ask for our prayers over her newborn baby. It was May 17, 2011. She managed to get my cell phone number from my aunt. She asked Rick and I to come to the hospital to pray over her sick baby. Of course, we went. We felt honored she reached out to us, and we felt hopeful this might be our opportunity to share God's love with her and assist in the healing of her newborn. Perhaps this was the avenue God would use to draw her to Him.

On May 18, we arrived at the hospital in downtown Sacramento. We were not prepared for what we walked into.

I'm not sure what shocked me the most, the way my cousin looked from years of drug use and living on the streets, or the way she nonchalantly welcomed us into her hospital room as if we were her best friends. From the looks we received from the nurses, we knew they wondered who we were and what we were doing there. At the time, we were unaware of her outrages toward the nurses over the previous forty-eight hours.

My heart broke. I remembered my cousin as a healthy little girl. Seeing the toll of the drugs on her life almost brought me to tears. I never imagined this being a reality in my own family. I was reminded that day that drugs spare no one. They wreak havoc, ruin lives, and create brokenness. Now detoxing from methamphetamines, my cousin suffered with severe withdrawals. Her behavior was both frightening and sad. I had no experience walking alongside someone detoxing. I stood unprepared for the outbursts of emotional anger, physical pains, chills, shaking, impulse control, and the spiritual chaos of a demonic presence. It was all there. It was ugly, hard, and so sad. My heart broke when I realized the depths of her depravity. All I wanted to do was help her get better.

We prayed for her, and we were escorted into the NICU. We met her nine-pound fifteen-ounce baby boy hooked to oxygen, heart machines, and a morphine drip. Rhythmic beeps and sounds of hospital monitors filled the room. Baby Jason fought for his life. He, too, was detoxing. A

sudden withdrawal would cause an immediate heart failure, so the morphine drip helped manage the rate of his
detox. He lay there comatose, his face covered with large
tubes taped over his mouth and others entering his nose.
We held his little hands as we prayed so many prayers.

We learned Jason received no prenatal care and was exposed to so many drugs in utero without his nutritional
needs being met.

In an attempt to help my cousin get clean and sober,
we decided as a family to bring her home to our house
while we worked on getting her admitted into a rehabilitation center. We spent the next six weeks with her. We
drove her to and from the hospital twice a day to feed
baby Jason. We took her to appointments at the health
department, child welfare, the courthouse, and multiple
facilities that offered rehabilitation. We walked alongside
her during her recovery and felt hopeful she was on the
right track. With some effort, she was finally accepted
into a residential program—an answered prayer for all of
us. We did everything we could to help her find a new life
and make better choices.

I continued to visit Jason morning and night. I fell
deeply in love with the little guy. I rocked him to sleep
in the evenings and prayed over him daily. I trusted God
to heal him, and to reunite him with his mommy. We felt
sure she was on the right track but learned a few days after
we dropped her off at rehab, she left the program. She was
no longer visiting the baby. She simply left. Disappeared.
Fighting the stronghold of addiction proved too much for
her, and she returned to the drugs. This was the only way

she knew how to cope, and it was heartbreaking to watch. We cried. We felt devastated for her, for Jason, and for the brokenness that would need to be pieced back together.

After six weeks, Jason began breathing on his own. He received a feeding tube, surgically placed. At this stage in Jason's healing and growth, the doctors thought a stable home environment and a family was the best thing for the twelve-pound baby boy. A hospital social worker took custody of Jason and placed him as a ward of the court. As soon as this happened, we received a call from the social worker.

"Wendi, we have some news. Jason is ready to be dismissed from the hospital, and he will be going into foster care. His medical team has recommended placement with your family, if it's possible. He has already bonded with you, and we believe there can be so much more healing if he were being held and loved. We think the constant attention from a large family would be really good for him."

My heart dropped, and I cried again. We had nothing prepared to take in a six-week-old infant. I didn't know how to care for a medically fragile baby. His file was large, messy, and complicated. His biological mom is someone I love dearly. I hoped, helped, prayed, and poured into her, believing for a different outcome. We were told, "Jason may have cerebral palsy, he is lethargic, and may never walk or talk." He was officially labeled "failure to thrive."

Saying yes to our second adoption meant we were willing to pray for physical healing, but we were also willing to trust God's grace if healing was not in the near future. Saying yes meant, no matter what, Jason became our son, and we would love him unconditionally, forever and ever. This was one of the most faith-filled yeses we ever made. We prayed as a family. All five of our children had a say in the matter. We wanted them to know how different our lives could look. We wanted them to know that I would be gone a lot at doctors' appointments. Jason would have a feeding tube. People would stare at us. He would have multiple medical appointments a week. He might never walk. Everything would change. This would be a very hard yes.

Just as with our adoption with Neb, our children were so full of childlike faith they questioned me. "Why wouldn't we take Jason?" They knew the risks, and they still gave a strong, confident YES! We are so glad they did. Our village became so energized.

I felt terrified for so many reasons, but mostly because I don't do well with medical emergencies. Not. At. All. It's so bizarre, but when I become super anxious when someone is hurt, I often respond with a laughing episode. I'm not laughing at the hurt person. I know the situation isn't funny, but my nerves respond in the opposite manner. I laugh rather than panic.

The night of July 4, 2011, I was not laughing. When they welcomed me to the room where Jason and I would be staying, I quickly realized they placed us outside the walls of the Natal Intensive Care Unit. No nurses. No security guards. Full access to the public. I felt uncomfortable using a feeding tube and medical machines by myself even though I knew nurses worked beyond the double doors less than twenty feet away. They kindly taught me everything I needed to know about using the tube as they moved Jason's NICU crib into the family room, where we stayed overnight.

Typically, this particular week was the one weekend each year Rick and I traveled to a beautiful campsite to celebrate Fourth of July as a family. Cornhole, s'mores, swimming, fire pits, and family time always equal July 4th, but not this year. This year my family camped as usual, but I stayed in the hospital preparing to bring our medically fragile baby home from the hospital the following day.

The sun set. Night fell. Fireworks began. I listened to their muffled crackles and explosions from the confines of the hospital room. I grieved yet again. Since she left the rehab, I desperately tried to reach Jason's biological mom, and failed each time. She had not responded. I was angry, but not at her. Disappointed, yes. But I was angry at the drugs that gripped the lives of those we love, angry at sin, and angry at Satan. I was angry that "Plan A" for Jason to be with his biological mom became impossible. I cried as I prayed to God for answers. Sleep evaded me all night, but finally, my cousin called. The first contact since she left rehab, and I immediately knew she was not on the right track. Her demeanor flipped from once receiving all our love to rejecting it. She made some harsh accusations on the phone that night, and she didn't at all support us in taking Jason. She threatened me for the first time, and a real sense of fear washed over me.

I already felt fearful taking care of Jason, but her threat heightened my fear. Would she hurt me? Would she show up? I explained with as much love and grace within me that she could always be a part of his life if she was clean and sober. I told her how much we loved her. I said she still had time to get help and that we would support her. I spoke the truths I knew, but she was too angry to receive any of it. She hung up the phone. Emotionally exhausted, I reclined on the hospital chair, staring at the ceiling in fear while my family looked up at the open sky enjoying fireworks while camping. As I glanced upward, I asked God to take away the fear. The motto I lived and currently live by is, "Do it afraid." We were doing just that.

Like my children, I had said yes to adopting Jason. It was our final answer. I believe this is always how our yes must look. A faith-filled confident yes is trusting and knowing God will walk us right through the unknowns. And, if the diagnosis is true, and walking is impossible, knowing He will carry us through. Either way, deep faith with God will always get us to the other side—and for Neb and Jason, deep faith will get you home.

5

HOME SWEET HOME

"For we know that if the earthly tent we live in is destroyed, we have a building from God, and eternal house in heaven, not built by human hands" (2 Corinthians 5:1).

Staying Home

Each morning, as I dropped Colby at daycare, he clung to me, cried the most heart-wrenching tears, and called my name repeatedly, ripping my heart out with each plea. He was not even two years old, but my teaching career flourished so quickly after college I couldn't possibly pass up an immediate job offer. After my student teaching ended mid-school year, our principal, one of my heroes, offered me a full-time teaching position. She saw the passion and work ethic of this young teacher, and she knew I would give it my all.

I did just that. I gave it all I had. I was too young and driven to slow down long enough to realize the most important people in my life, my new husband and my precious baby, were getting the very worst of me. Exhausted from the one hour commute each morning and afternoon, the long days of teaching little children, and the constant lesson-planning, I had little left to give. I meant well, and I was doing everything I thought I had dreamed of.

Being the first college graduate in my family, and the first to land a "real" career, I considered myself successful. I had arrived, so I thought. However, soon after beginning my job, the time commitment began to take a serious toll on me. I remember driving down the highway dozing off, looking in my rearview mirror, seeing Colby's little face fast asleep, and slapping myself to stay awake. I was coming and going in the dark. I left the house each morning before the sun rose and returned home long after sunset. The first couple of years teaching require so much planning and preparation.

On top of that, I agreed to participate in a principal mentorship program which required me to create grade-standard Excel sheets and facilitate workshops after school for the other teaching staff. I outworked myself constantly, unable to stop.

Thirteen-hour days became the norm. I left my house at 5:30 a.m. to arrive in my class by 7 a.m. I taught the entire day, stayed for prep and planning, taught a workshop, met with parents, made copies, shopped for supplies, and the list goes on. As long as I reached daycare by 6 p.m. to pick-up Colby, the childcare prices were covered. It hurts my heart to even look back on this style of work. I'm beyond grateful God's grace is sufficient. Although Colby cried and reached for me as I walked back to my car, I stuffed down the feelings of sadness and pulled up my bootstraps. I convinced myself I was right where I was supposed to be because I was helping twenty-eight kids. If I were to stay home, I would only be helping one. I never stopped to ask God if I was in His will because I assumed my new teaching career was most definitely a God thing.

This is a great place to pause and thank all the teachers out there who are reading this now and can relate to the countless hours of work. You are appreciated, needed, and seen. Thank you!

Colby, under two years old, struggled to stay healthy for any length of time. It always started with a cold, runny nose, and fever, then morphed into croup cough that led to severe asthma and/or infections. The breathing treatments sometimes offered temporary relief, only for Colby to end up back in the hospital. The infections came so often it forced me to take off work, and poor Colby suffered countless blood draws. The medical staff even checked his blood for leukemia. The medical staff was stumped. They hadn't seen a little guy like Colby get sick so often without finding a severe disease.

When summer arrived, I breathed a sigh of relief. For at least a couple of months I would be home with Colby. At that time, he was healthy, and the season for croup cough had passed. I began meeting with a neighbor weekly for Bible study. She beautifully modeled her role as a stay-at-home mom. I admired the way she menu-planned, gathered family, hosted dinners, and facilitated play dates. I enjoyed watching her teach her kids Bible stories and play outside with them. I started wondering what it would be like if I stayed home with Colby. I struggled to wrap my head around the possibility, and saw it more as a fantasy—a pipe dream.

Only three months had passed since I lost our second baby to a miscarriage. Colby was nearing three years old. How was this all going to work? I had a sick baby, a deceased baby, and somehow, I was supposed to be putting my hope in this "new" Christian life meant to "prosper and not harm you."

Well, I felt harmed. You bet I did. I questioned God, hard, and I didn't let up. I needed to know why He allowed all the bad in my life while I was trying to be good. I spent hours and hours in prayer, seeking answers from God to hard questions. I imagine, in my interrogation, God hearing me, listening patiently.

The doctors told me, after my ectopic surgery, that I would have a very difficult time getting pregnant again. They gave me a 50 percent chance. In my Christian childhood, I spewed out a "fleece" to God. Like Gideon in the Bible, I too lacked faith. I bargained with the Lord. "God, if I can get pregnant again, I will stay home with my babies and take a break from my teaching career." More than my aspiration of being a teacher, I dreamed of being a mom. Watching my neighbor, Catherine, with her family showed me how very much I desired that. I feared Colby would be our only child, so I made a promise to God. I later learned that promise would be hard to keep.

The first time Rick and I were allowed to be intimate after my surgery, and the week after I spewed out my fleece before God, I conceived. It was that miraculous! To me, that was the voice of God. "Here you go, be a mom.

Stay home with your babies. I give you the desires of your heart, and home is where your heart is." It was not the audible voice of God I heard, but it was an ever-present peace. I knew it was confirmation. Home. That's where I would predominately camp out for the next season of my life. Home sweet home never meant so much. It sounds cliché, but there really is no place like home.

Airport Angel

The traveling aspect of getting home proved difficult for Neb. We saw the joy and excitement fade to fear and confusion, but we didn't know why. I thought perhaps he was unhappy about the adoption, and he didn't want to leave Ethiopia after all. My insecurities crept in the farther we traveled away from all he had ever known. His smile slowly disappeared. On Ethiopian Airlines the flight attendant spoke his language, and the foods served were all the common meals he was accustomed to. He seemed to be excited about coming home with us, and the first few hours went smoothly. The familiarity of the language and the food he experienced on the first leg of the flight helped. However, he began to look downcast when he awoke from sleeping six hours during our flight. When we exited the plane in Washington, DC. Rick and I assumed he was hungry. Colby couldn't wait to buy his new big brother a Frosty and French fries from Wendy's during our layover.

Neb's legs shook in terror as we rode the first escalator up to the food court. Having never seen such a thing, it must have felt to him like a magic carpet ride. We continued our best to read his mood, but he seemed to be growing more and more downcast. When Colby handed him the French fries, he shook his head with a very confident, "No." At that moment, I began to pray. I convinced myself Neb was unhappy about being in our family and wanted desperately to return to Ethiopia. Neb and I left Wendy's to find a chair to sit on while we waited for Rick and Colby to devour their first American meal in two weeks.

I couldn't shake the burden I was feeling, so I did all I knew how to do. Pray. I asked God to help me communicate with Neb. I prayed for discernment to know what was wrong and how I could help. I sat there feeling desperate and waited. Only moments after I opened my eyes, an employee from the airport walked up to us. He was a beautiful man. He looked familiar and friendly. He had the same skin tone as Neb, and they shared similar facial features. He glanced at Neb. Then he cut a glance at me, "Is this your son?"

I replied with a very quick, "Yes, we are just coming home and…" only to be interrupted by the man.

"You adopted him from Ethiopia?"

"Yes," I replied with obvious insecurity. "He isn't happy, and I do not know what is wrong."

"May I speak to him?"

"Of course."

And the conversation began. Neb's eyes lit up like the Fourth of July when he heard his native language for the first time in hours. I saw the relief well up in his eyes, his demeanor change, and his head lift with confidence. I listened closely yet understood nothing. I waited for the man to tell me what I feared, assuming Neb wanted to go back, and I braced for bad news when the man started interpreting Neb's words.

"Your son is very sick from the airplane. The smell of any food makes him feel like he will throw up. He doesn't want to eat, but he doesn't want you to think he is being a bad boy. If you walk down this hall there is a kiosk down that way, and they sell Dramamine. Please get that for your son before the next flight, and it will help him through. Also, in case you are thinking he isn't happy about being adopted, he told me how his prayers were answered, and he is flying home with his forever family. Thank you for going to my country and helping my people."

With that, the man walked away, but I chased him down for a big hug. I knew it was God who answered my prayers, but I also recognized that man as an airport angel. I bought the Dramamine, Neb chewed it, and out he went. He slept during the remaining flights home, and even passed out in the long car ride home from the airport. He was still groggy when we pulled up to our home, but the excitement and joy of meeting his baby sister, Cami, woke him right up. All Neb ever wanted was a forever family, but he specifically prayed for a baby sister. He walked in, swooped Cami up in his arms and began kissing her cheeks. Still to this day Neb kisses babies' cheeks. If only everyone could see him with his first nephew, Cash, his niece Haven, and his very own baby girl, Elyana. A welcome home greeting at our home could very well be a kiss!

I like to imagine what our welcome home party will look like when we walk through the pearly gates. Will it be full of joy, excitement, and a forever family?

I believe there will be brothers and sisters of all ages and colors. Although our home here is full, beautiful, and blessed, we know it is our temporary residence. Until we meet Jesus face-to-face in our eternal home, we must keep our hope grounded in Him. We must embrace the love and laughter of family, gather in community, grow in relationships, and build our homes on solid ground.

When we do this, we place all our faith in knowing there is more. There is an eternal abode where we will be welcomed with perfect love, perfect hospitality, and perfect joy. When we believe in Jesus, we too have been adopted into the family of God, and someday we will return "home." It will be a glorious day. Just as Neb was welcomed with open arms, we too will be embraced. The perfect love of our Father welcomes us!

6

ESL: ENGLISH AS A
SECOND LANGUAGE

*"Dear children, let us not love with words or speech
but with actions and truth"* (1 John 3:18).

Cookie

It takes humility to be submersed in an English-speaking family and country when you speak no English. "Coooooo-keeee," he yelled into the microphone. Again, but louder, "Coooooo-keeeeee!" Over and over, louder and louder, "Coooooo-keeeee," but his thick accent was not changing.

He listened, repeated it, and couldn't understand why it would not pass onto the next word. The first four weeks he was with us, Neb spent most of his days with Rosetta Stone. Multiple social workers and adoptive parents encouraged us to keep Neb home for a while, and not enroll him in school immediately. The idea was to help Neb acclimate to his new environment and to allow a time for family bonding. The attachment process in adoption can be rather tricky, often sensitive, and sometimes outright impossible. Thankfully, in both of our adoption stories, we have been able to form healthy attachments. That is not always the case.

We have had dear friends experience the opposite journeys, and to this day, struggle with Reactive Attachment Disorder (RAD). RAD "is a rare but serious condition in which an infant or young child doesn't establish healthy attachments with parents or caregivers."[1] Although this is rare, it is very familiar to many in the foster and adoption community. These are real issues for adoptive families, and they are painful. The foster/adoption classes work to prepare families for this. When people step out in faith to adopt, they naturally hope, pray, and expect to love and be loved. The reality is that it is unfair to expect a broken person to return affection. Often, all we can do is care for them. Unconditional love expects nothing in return. My heart aches for those who have adopted and struggled with attachment. It's heartbreaking. I am aware of this struggle and pray for those who face it. If this is your experience, please know you are not alone, and this is not your fault. Persevere. Endure. And lean into the loving arms of Jesus, the One who knows what it is like to be rejected by those you love.

But as Neb attached to us, he persevered in learning English. While Neb worked hard to learn English, we had to find a way to communicate. One way we did this

---

1 "Reactive Attachment Disorder." Mayo Clinic. Last modified May 12, 2022. https://www.mayoclinic.org/diseases-conditions/reactive-attachment-disorder/symptoms-causes/syc-20352939#.

was through his journal. Neb wrote every morning. He wrote in Amharic, so we needed help to understand it, but this method worked well for us.

Adoption takes help. Going at it alone is not a great plan for success. It helped that the elementary school my children attended at the time was multicultural and super supportive of our adoption. What a blessing! When we shared with the principal about our adoption, she immediately connected us with an Ethiopian family who attended the school. This family owned an Ethiopian restaurant in Sacramento. It became a frequent stop, and not just for food. Neb and I went there weekly for lunch and the employees helped by reading his journal and interpreting for me. This activity helped me learn Neb's desire to be in school with his siblings.

School in Africa is a privilege. It is not free, and so many kids whose families cannot pay school fees sit outside the fence peering in, wishing they were inside those gates. I have seen this with my own eyes over the years. Our family learned that education could change the cycle of poverty for an entire family. We learned that in Africa many biological aunties and uncles, grandmas and grandpas, and even village neighbors would care for orphans if they could afford to send them to school. This is how our education program at xHope first began. We selected ten children from the local church who were living with loving parents but who couldn't send them to school. We took pictures and came home to share their stories with our friends. We found ten sponsor families and began sending these children to school.

Now, some of those children have graduated from university and are politicians, engineers, social workers, and staff at our children's home. It's an investment that has reaped so much fruit. I only wish we had a sponsor for every waiting child!

Neb wasn't thrilled to be "waiting" to go to school in America. He didn't understand why I kept him home and sent his brothers to school. I asked the waitress at the Ethiopian Restaurant to explain to Neb that he needed to learn English before I sent him to school. I was not keeping him out because he was in trouble or not smart enough. I wanted us to properly attach to each other. I desired for him to understand some English on his first day of sixth grade. He never did understand the attachment thing, but he clearly understood he had to learn English. Once this clicked, I couldn't get him off Rosetta Stone. He started flying through the lessons. He spent hours on the computer, headset on, working endlessly to get through all the lessons. Sometimes he would say the words correctly, but the dialect was wrong, and so a red X would appear on the screen.

When this happened, he would try again. And again. And again. Sometimes I heard him repeating the same word louder and louder ten to fifteen times. Think about times when you've tried to get someone to understanding what you're saying, but somehow, they don't understand. Instead of changing the word, you yell louder. We've all done that.

I often listened from my room and gave Neb the space he needed to work. I appeared only after the tone of his voice changed from determination to straight frustration. Much like the day he tried to say, "cookie." I walked in, put my right hand on his shoulder, looked at the computer, and whispered into his microphone, "Cookie." This always resulted in a big green check across the screen, and the program passed him onto the next word. It was always a relief to him when I came in and saved the day.

As parents, I think we are always trying to decide when to let our kids persevere, when to let them fall, and when to step in and show grace. A simple whisper of the word "cookie" was all it took to let Neb know I was right there. Sometimes we all need that tap on the shoulder, a gentle whisper, and perhaps a little milk to go with that "Coooooo-keeeee."

Bath Time for All

"Wohooooooo," Neb yelled from the bathroom as the waterspout turned on then immediately off. "Wohoooooo," he shouted again, and the water went from full blast to dry as a bone.

We sat by the door, ears pressed like pancakes in hopes of hearing exactly what was going on in there. Neb's first shower with running water turned into an adventure. It was his first night in his new home with his new family and his new pajamas. Long days of travel, motion sickness, and a whole new world for Neb. In Ethiopia, bathing was done in a basin, with about three gallons of water from the spout and a bar of soap. The weather outside determined the temperature of the bath water in the small basin. There was no shower, no running water, and no spout spewing an unending flow of hot water. It was then we realized Neb didn't know how to work the running water. He didn't understand what was hot and what was cold. He didn't know he could leave the water running and we wouldn't run out of water. Neb had been taught all his life the value of water. He knew what it meant to not waste resources. Water was life, and he wouldn't dare use up all of ours.

Our entire family gathered around the bathroom door at 10 p.m. trying to problem-solve the issue we knew Neb faced. We showed him how to turn the water on, how to turn it off, and everything in between. We hoped he would figure it out. We assumed he would sit under the shower and use the bar of soap to scrub clean. We hoped he would enjoy this wonderful luxury we have in America. Instead, he was quite nervous about it all. As he continued to turn the water on, then off, and make noise effects each time, our family contemplated the issue.

"I think it's too hot for him," Colby said.

"No, buddy, he is trying to save water because he thinks it will run out," Rick said.

Casey weighed in. "I think it's too cold."

"I take bath, too," Cami suggested in her little toddler voice.

"No, you're a girl. You can't take a bath with Neb," said Cooper.

"Rick, what should we do?" I hissed. "We can't just let him figure it out, and I can't go in there. He's a twelve-year-old boy."

On and on we discussed this dilemma, trying to analyze

the situation, when Casey came up with a brilliant idea. "How about all the brothers get on swimsuits, we take Neb his swim shorts, and we take a bath together?"

"Yes!" Colby's face lit up with excitement, thrilled with his brother's idea. Before we could respond, the three boys raced to their bedrooms, threw off their clothes, and ran back, ready for bath time. Neb froze with a "deer-in-the-headlights" look when three boys opened the door and converged in the bathroom all at once. They covered their eyes like three little monkeys trying not to impose on Neb's privacy. Colby handed Neb his shorts, and they all jumped in the tub. Cami, Rick, and I listened by the door as the boys coached Neb about all things shower, bath, and running water. They showed him how to turn the handle left for hot, right for cold, up for on, and down for off. They showed him what to do with bar soap and a washcloth. Colby used the face wash, then Neb copied his movements. They showed him that the blue and white bottle was shampoo, and they squirted it in his hair. They showed him how to pull up the silver lever for the shower to turn on, they rinsed their hair, and then demonstrated how to push the lever back down for the shower to turn off. We finally heard them explain how to plug and drain the bath. I'll always treasure this memory as one of the sweetest moments I can remember—all four brothers, ages twelve, eleven, seven, and five, bathing together in their swimsuits.

They played "charades" for a long time, practicing all they taught him. They used the shower, and all began laughing as Neb splashed about, flinging the water as it rained down continuously on him. Joy was abundant, and we were yet again reminded of God's grace. As they were winding down bath time, aka impromptu pool party, we heard them laughing, giggling, splashing, and counting out loud to see who could hold their breath the longest.

As they were holding their breath, Rick and I breathed a sigh of relief. We knew no matter the language we spoke, the country we were born in, or the color of our skin, we were family, and these boys were 100 percent committed to being with Neb every step of his adjustment into our family. The language would come later, but the love came immediately.

Soccer Is a Universal Language

He didn't speak English yet. However, soccer is considered a universal language. Neb joined the competitive soccer team with his new brother, Colby. Being in America for a short six weeks didn't stop Neb from trying new things. His self-confidence on the outside made him the perfect candidate to "adapt" to this new team.

We didn't realize, at the time, how incredibly confusing it was for Neb, who spoke Amharic, to live with his new family who spoke English, and to be coached by two Hispanic men who talked in fluent Spanish. Neb didn't seem to mind and joined the team as if he was born to play. He worked hard and was usually on task.

In fact, those off-task on his team were "rewarded" with team pushups.

Each time a player didn't respond as told by the coach, didn't meet the timeline, or shoot the ball as directed, the whole team was disciplined with a set of pushups. The way this would unfold was simple. "Nope, everyone drop, pushups," the coach would holler out.

The boys immediately dropped to the ground, counted aloud in unison for each pushup until they completed twenty. I thought to myself, *This is great. At least he is learning to count in English.*

It wasn't until the very first game that we all realized this language barrier had created serious confusion.

Colby and Neb awoke with excitement as they dressed for their very first soccer match. Without words, Colby showed Neb the correct way to wear his uniform, socks, and cleats. They filled water bottles and loaded up the soccer gear. Their anticipation grew during the forty-minute drive. They talked and laughed the entire time even though Neb had no clue what Colby said. He giggled like a schoolgirl because he was so happy. Neb was thrilled to finally play organized soccer.

The barefoot soccer played in Ethiopia with a ball made of cornstalks was just enough to pique his interest and keep him physically fit. Having done soccer barefoot, Neb had the confidence of a pro baller in his brand-new Nike cleats. The boys hustled out to the beautiful green soccer field and lined up to stretch with their team. They completed their organized warm-up and began taking shots on the goal. They ran a few laps, and the captains took their places in the middle of the field for the coin toss. "Heads," Neb's team called. Atlas started with the ball. Coach positioned Neb as middle defender, and he sat back in his position as best he could.

The anticipation killed him. All he really wanted to do was run around chasing that ball, like he played soccer in Ethiopia. Even so, Neb learned how important it was to stay in his position. He knew if he didn't, he would sit on the bench. He stayed. However, his goalie began to direct him, pointing where he wanted Neb to go.

"Over!" Neb followed directions. That went well, until the goalie yelled a command that had multiple meanings.

"Neb, push up!"

Suddenly, in the middle of a very competitive soccer game, Neb dropped to the ground doing pushups, counting aloud, "One, two, three…"

The laughter on the sidelines echoed as my husband called to him.

"Neb, GET UP!

With total frustration he got up, stomped his cleats, waved his hand in the air, and yelled back at the sidelines with very broken English.

"What? Goalie say for me to push up. He say that," as he pointed to the goalie with anger. "It's his fault!" Frustrated, like a two-year-old child. The language barrier we experienced had a whole new meaning for us, Neb, and his Hispanic coaches. So is soccer really a universal language after all?

Being embarrassed as a child can lead to a great story of laughter later in life, as this one has, but being humiliated as a child can also lead to pain and insecurities. Neb struggled with that for years, but eventually understood there is no gain without a little pain.

7

LOSS AND HEARTBREAK

*"Praise be to God and Father of our Lord Jesus
Christ, The Father of compassion and the God of all
comfort, who comforts us in all our troubles, so that
we can comfort those in any trouble with the comfort
we receive from God"* (2 Corinthians 1:3-4).

Miscarriage

As I drove myself to the Principal Mentorship class I had
been chosen to attend, I prayed and prayed the cramping
would go away. It was such an honor for my principal to
have hand selected me. Of all the teachers desiring this
path, she chose me. The cramps worsened. I called my
teaching partner, whose father was a pharmacist in my
small town, and asked, "What can your dad give me for
the worst cramps ever?"

"Nothing," she said, "go to the ER."

But I couldn't. I would disappoint the principal of my
school, the one who hand-picked me out of eighty-five
other staff members, to fast-track me to becoming an

administrator. She was my mentor and had invested so much in me. I looked up to her. Her achievements, leadership, and drive inspired me. I attended the workshop with her, and I decided as soon as it was over, I would go to the ER if the cramping persisted. I was eager to learn from another principal in the district, but I didn't last. I doubled over after being there for only thirty minutes, so I drove myself to the hospital. The pain became so severe, it was impossible to ignore, much less endure. All alone, in severe agony, I left a quick message for my husband telling him I was on my way to the emergency room. I arrived at the hospital, still optimistic. I felt sure the issue was my appendix. I had seen appendicitis as a child when my brother went in for surgery. Again, I witnessed it as an adult when my husband went in for surgery. Despite the pain, I didn't feel fear because I knew having your appendix removed was a common, quick, outpatient surgery.

Before I could contact anyone other than my husband, the medical staff began preparations for emergency surgery. I learned our second baby, whom we prayed for, was in my fallopian tube and it had burst. Had I waited an entire day, I could have died. I was grateful I didn't delay. Although relieved I would be okay, I was absolutely devastated to learn my baby would not survive. I wondered, as the lights faded and my eyes closed for surgery, *Is it a boy or girl? Should I name her/him? Will I ever get pregnant again?*

These musings haunted me as I drifted off to sleep for surgery. They remained in my thoughts for many nights. I tried to escape the feelings of loss and talk myself into believing I shouldn't need to grieve since it was so early in the pregnancy. At only five weeks, most people don't even know they are pregnant. Surely, since I didn't even know I was expecting, I should brush it off and move forward, right?

Wrong.

I did what I knew how to do when grief-stricken. I cried some tears alone, in secret. When asked how I was doing, I replied with a very cheerful, "I'm fine." I was a brand-new Christian when this loss occurred. So, I did what most believers do. I asked, "Why God?"

I had never heard the voice of God. I thought people who shared testimony about how God spoke to them were a little off their rockers. I was turned off by the cliché, "I heard God..." Often, I would callously think to myself that hearing from God meant His booming, loud voice spoken audibly. I thought people who said they heard God were full of it. Of course, I talked to God. I prayed. I asked all the questions. This was what I thought was normal for Christians. At least for *baby believers* like me. But I was missing a critical part of the equation, the hearing and listening part. I had not heard God, even though I did a lot of talking and questioning.

The voice of God became clearer to me over the years of reading His word. Because His Word *is* His voice, the more scripture I read, the more aware I became. As I continued to grow in my relationship with God, I began to recognize His still, small voice in times of prayer, in music, in creation, and through people. His voice can be a nudge. It can be a dream. It can be a scripture or a sermon.

Although I have yet to hear the audible voice of God, I do know when He is speaking to me.

The Village Bar

When you hear God's voice, it's natural that you ask him more questions. It's common, normal, and acceptable to talk to God about our queries. He wants us to! When we do not ask, we will often make up stories in our minds and believe those as truth. Have you ever misinterpreted a situation and found yourself fearful? This happened to me the first night we visited Covenant Orphanage in Ethiopia.

Yelling, chanting, and obnoxious noises kept me up through the night. I laid with my eyes wide open in terror. Because this was our mission team's first trip to Ethiopia, we spent time researching before the trip. We were concerned for our safety. We knew to stay within the gates of the children's home, especially at night, and we heard animal sacrifices occurred regularly in the villages. We learned about the common use of witchcraft. Also, we were told of inhumane ways witch doctors perform rituals on children to heal them, all the while torturing them.

Anxiety began to kick in. I convinced myself the noises I heard were a child or animal sacrifice. I couldn't sleep. I didn't sleep. My anxiety influenced my mind. An entire story formed in my mind. I prayed all night and begged God to spare the child's life. Six hours of intended sleep felt like three days of fear. I couldn't rest at all. Early the next morning, we arose to the sounds of roosters crowing. Our host asked me, "How did you sleep?" I hesitated. I truly didn't mind sleeping on the floor in the girl's dorm and felt so blessed by their hospitality.

Despite the stories of inhumane sacrifices, we also learned of their amazing culture of hospitality, the beautiful coffee ceremonies, and the large Christian community loving orphans and widows. This was all so true. We were welcomed into the community of selfless, Jesus-loving staff at Covenant Orphanage. The children there were well-taken care of, from clothing to meals. The most overwhelming care was the shepherding from Pastor Busabi and orphanage director, Pochi.

Pastor Busabi was a very influential man, his smile and gentle touch always welcoming. His voice, bold and courageous, often speaking truth as if scripture were his only language. He came to visit the children multiple times a week. He was a father figure to the children and the first man in their lives who loved them unconditionally. He was available. Compassionate. Consistent. Loving. Most of all, he spoke into their lives in the deepest and most broken places. He showed them the love of God so they would someday believe in the love of God. He taught scripture and led worship. The kids prayed nightly together and woke up early in the mornings to be back on their knees for prayer.

Pochi was on-site most days overseeing the home, building relationships with the children, and encouraging the staff. She had full-time caretakers, but that didn't stop her from being a mother figure to all the children. Her job was to receive the children from the streets, confirm they were truly orphans, and in need. She filed paperwork, scheduled missionary visits, enrolled children in school, and kept the children's home up and running flawlessly. It was actually Pochi who worked side-by-side with Neb's sister, Kedija, to gain the government's permission to allow Neb into the orphanage. She told me many times she knew Neb would grow up to be a leader and a Jesus-follower. She believed his testimony would be used to encourage other children who experienced great loss. Pochi was right. Even now as I write, I smile and nod. Those who care for the orphans and widows are doing exactly what God has asked each of us to do, and those people get to influence these children and spark life into their grieving hearts.

The subconscious story conjured in my mind as I listened to the night long sounds, drove me just crazy enough to finally blurt out my answer.

"I really didn't rest because I heard the sacrifice last night and it was too hard for me."

"What do you mean? What did you hear?"

"The hollering and screaming. It was a large crowd gathered, and they would all burst into chants at the same time. Couldn't you hear it?"

Pochi began to giggle and shake her head with kindness as not to embarrass me.

"That sacrifice was one pro futbol team losing to another pro futbol team." She went on to explain, "That is the village bar behind the livestock, and men gather there all night long to tune into the futbol match. This is the only place in the village with a television. The games are held on American time zone, which means all night long. The hollering and screaming happened each time a goal was scored. We've gotten used to it. We sleep right through it."

That was a relief!

However, even though the bar was not a place of animal sacrifices as I had vividly imagined, by the sounds of it, it was a place for which men sacrificed their families. I learned many years later that same bar celebrating a futbol game was the place Neb often went with his biological dad.

This was the place five-year-old Neb tried alcohol for the first time, the place where his dad would spend the much-needed grocery money, the place where only men were allowed, and ultimately the place that served the deadly portions of alcohol which caused his liver to fail. As the dark, thick liquid was served to Neb in a bar glass, he politely refused. Although hungry and thirsty, he knew it was a drink for adults only. He also understood, from frequenting the bar with his dad, that the dark, thick liquid made some men do mean things. He knew the town drunks walked around sipping that drink. Eventually, it caused them to swear at the kids, switch them with sticks, and otherwise abuse them.

Neb was on the receiving end of this abuse and remembers a swift kick in the face. Once, his dad insisted he drink the liquid and so he did. After that, he fell fast asleep on the dirt floor. Neb woke from this drunkenness, but most men frequenting that bar lived in a state of inebriation. Choosing that bar was indeed a sacrifice, just not the one I created in my head that night.

Shiny Shoes

Drinking in that bar was not the only time Neb fell to the dirt floor. He was hungry, so hungry. It had been days since he and his sister had eaten. All he wanted was a small piece of injera and a tomato. Two items that cost around ten cents American money could feed a child on the streets and keep them alive. It seems so simple to us, but to Neb and his sister, and the nearly 600,000 estimated street kids country-wide in Ethiopia, the struggle was real.

There was no way for a child to earn ten cents unless neighbors in the village were feeling selfless enough to share what little they had. In fact, Nebeyu's biological mom, who worked in the market selling those same fresh tomatoes, would sit on a mat in the hot sunlight surrounded by the dry dirt for sixteen hours a day in hopes of making $1.

Ethiopia's average income is less than $1 dollar a day, but in order to have shelter, food, and water, they needed to sell the produce. Because it was impossible for Neb and Kedija to be on the receiving end of fresh produce, they had to beg, scavenge through rubbish, and ask for jobs from untrustworthy people.

There were times when prayers were answered. Neb's mother had friends who welcomed them into their homes for a meal. One neighbor took it upon herself to watch over Neb. She promised Neb's mom, while she was on her deathbed, that she would care for him.

Wrikensh did her best yet had very little herself. She

had a home, coffee, and bread to share. Neb remembers the days when he felt like dying. The moments he wanted to give up, to die and go to heaven with his mom. He remembers it was always in the most desperate of times that Wrikensh would gather him and his sister and bring them home with her. Opening her gates felt like entering heaven. Neb felt the love of his mother, their hunger relieved, and the scent of warm tea smelled like normalcy. God used Wrikensh to meet physical and emotional needs, and to Neb, she was a guardian angel.

Wrikensh couldn't provide food daily even though she wanted to. It had been a long day. Neb knew the man calling him over had visited the bar frequently. He could smell the liquor on his breath as the man demanded that six-year-old Neb shine his shoes. He passed Neb the black cloth and can of polish, and he sat on his chair. As Neb kneeled scrubbing hard to make the shoes shiny black and to appear brand new by rubbing away the scuffs and dust, the man made a promise. The vow was enough to keep Neb engaged. He promised Neb a piece of bread. This bread meant another day of life for Neb and his sister. His mouth was watering, thinking about the texture and taste of fresh bread. The two-day hunger pains subsided as his mind wandered. With every up and down, back and forth motion of the small brush, his mouth salivated.

The hard, humiliating work was worth it, if it meant he could feed himself and his sister. He scrubbed on. About an hour passed. Each time Neb looked up for approval, the intoxicated man shook his head in disapproval. No.

Neb wondered if he would ever meet the man's standards. He couldn't see a speck of dust left on the shoe, let alone a spot. Neb could practically see his face in the reflection of the shoe when he was sure there was no way to make them any cleaner.

Neb stood to his feet to stretch his muscle tight legs, and when he did, he was given a quick, swift kick to his face. He found himself yet again on the dirt ground, face throbbing, and still hungry. In anger, Neb hopped to his feet and did everything in his power to fight back. He was a helpless, starving child, struggling for what was right, the bread owed to him. He swung his arms and kicked his feet only to be snatched up like a rag doll and beaten badly. The little boy, doing all he knew how to do to earn food, was left hungry and battered once again.

Even a dog feels the difference between being kicked and tripped over. This episode left a scar on Neb's soul that has taken years to overcome.

8

MISSION IS
EVERYDAY LIFE

"The apostles said to the Lord, Increase our faith! He replied, "If you have faith as small as a mustard seed, you can say to this mulberry tree, 'be uprooted and planted in the sea,' and it will obey you" (Luke 17:5-6).

Soccer

The joke happened after our first soccer tournament with the Elk Grove Wolves. People jokingly started asking us, "Did you go to Ethiopia on a recruiting trip and bring back the best player you could find?" We promised we didn't do that, but God knew what He was planning when He brought Neb into our family. He so graciously gifted Colby with a soccer buddy for life and gifted us with a wonderful son. I believe God cares deeply about the details of our lives and the desires of our hearts.

It's been rather amazing to see the way soccer has been woven in and out of our adoption stories and found its way into the center of most mission trips.

WENDI CROSS

Soccer became a passion for Colby at the early age of three. He took to the sport early and dedicated every day to playing it. You rarely would find Colby anywhere without a soccer ball. He was so talented, even at age three, and would score goal after goal after goal. This passion only increased as he grew. He was committed to the sport, and so were we. This was an investment we were willing to make as a family because we believed Colby possessed pure talent for the sport. We were right. He ended up with a college scholarship to play.

During the year of fundraising for Neb's adoption, we felt compelled to take a break from competitive soccer. There were many factors that played into this, but mostly, we wanted the sacrifices we were making to adopt Neb to be done with everything we had.

We knew the adoption process would cost us nearly $30,000 and we only had $8,000 saved. We wanted to *go first* and use all our resources before applying for grants and hosting fundraising events. We did just that. We emptied our savings, and then sat down as a family and discussed our budget for the next year.

Cutting out competitive soccer and placing Colby on a recreational soccer team would save our family nearly $4,000, which could go directly toward the cost associated with adoption. Colby, at age eleven, agreed to take one year off. Competitive soccer is a full-time, year-around sport. The greatest blessing of this change was that Colby joined the most unbelievably talented, kind, and athletic team he had ever played on.

Although we stepped down from the top-ranked team,

88

the team he joined was ranked lower only because they played one season of soccer and another season of baseball. Not only was his new team incredible at soccer, but these families joined forces with us and gave financially toward our adoption. They volunteered at events, helped gather soccer jerseys, and followed our journey from start to finish. Many of these families sponsor our non-profit even today and support kids like Neb through xHope. The coaches on the Wolves team even went the extra mile and committed to saving our new son a spot on the team, regardless of his talent level. We were so proud to bring them a superstar. There were zero complaints.

We didn't bring Neb back in the athletic jumpsuit he wore nearly every day for three years, though the suit held a special place for Neb.

The Power of Gifts

John Dutton, our friend who brought Rick to Covenant Orphanage for his first mission trip, had gifted Neb a sports outfit. You know the kind, with the pants and jackets that match. Some call these warm-ups or jogging suits. When Rick met Neb for the first time, he was running around the front yard playing soccer in a pair of gray highwater pants and a matching gray zip-up jacket. Rick immediately noticed Neb's pants were three inches too short, but he assumed it was all the orphanages could afford. The truth was, Neb had a dresser full of clothes just his size, but that athletic outfit from John was his treasure.

He looked up to John for many reasons, mostly because John was there to teach sports ministry and disciple the kids in the word of God. John used his passion for sports, and his athletic giftings, to gather children all over the village. He taught, trained, and allowed them to compete. He was a coach and a father figure as he built relationships on and off the field. These friendships allowed John to earn trust and model love. He was being the hands and feet of Jesus, and lives were being transformed.

John and Neb formed a great connection. John called out Neb's leadership skills from the first time they met and treated Neb like the man of God he believed he would become. Their relationship mimicked a father-son relationship. When a father gifts something to a son, there is no growing out of that gift. Even three inches too short, to Neb, it still fit just right. It still amazes me something as small as an athletic suit could mean so much to a child like Neb. Small gifts are never insignificant, and we see the same blessing when things are given to the children we serve at Redeemer House.

I have left so many soccer jerseys, athletic suits, and dresses for the girls. Each time I return, the clothes are worn with gratitude and pride. I have the beautiful privilege of replacing these clothes every few months, thanks to so many of our partners, but even when they are swapped with new clothes the right size, the outfits that once fit them are given to children in the village who are not so fortunate. I wish we could gift every child there with a new athletic suit just like John did for Neb. I know getting a new outfit is a priceless act of love to those children and a very normal occurrence here.

We brought Neb a suitcase full of new clothes when we

went to pick him up. That was one year after Rick saw him in those short, gray athletic pants. Rick forewarned me of his attachment to the athletic suit and he would most likely be wearing it. He was!

However, when he saw his suitcase full of new clothes, he immediately began handing out his things to other kids at the orphanage. He even left that favorite gray suit to one of the younger boys. It has never been difficult for Neb to share anything. He knows what it is like to live with little and to love so much. I am so thankful all of my kids learned this type of selfless love by visiting Africa. Not only have they been on the giving end of mission, but they have received more love and life from going on mission than anything we have ever gifted them.

I have a friend who wrote a book called *Missionary Mom*.[1] She talks openly about our mission field being right inside our homes and in our neighborhoods. I agree with her. I have seen firsthand how starting in my home has allowed us as a family to spread our wings and become missionaries across the street and across the seas. We have learned how important it is to use the strengths, passions, and everyday tasks to lead us places where we can love others.

Soccer is a perfect example. As I stated, Colby began playing soccer at the age of three. If someone would have told me back then that he would one day use his passion for soccer to collect jerseys and deliver them to

---

1   Brewer, Shontelle. Missionary Mom: Embracing the Mission Field Right Under Your Roof. Kregel Publications, 2018.

Africa, I would have laughed. Never was Africa a part of our dreams or plans, but when our mission field started in our home and traveled all the way to Africa, I could only thank God for the opportunity and say, "Yes, send us." We continue to build, and they continue to come.

Miracles

In addition to answering God's opportunities, we have to be open to his miracles. I believe in miracles. I believe we see them daily if we look for them. God wants us praying for miracles and expecting them to come to pass. I encourage those around me to pray BIG, BOLD prayers. When we prepare our mission teams for Uganda, we hold very intentional mission training. At the end of this training, we ask each member of the team to journal a BIG, BOLD prayer to God.

My cousin Jacqui was taking her second trip to Uganda. She knew a bit about what to expect. She had not yet fully surrendered her life to Jesus Christ. She described herself as "spiritual," yet not fully surrendered to God. She was open to a relationship, but she didn't have one yet. On this particular trip, Jacqui shared her BIG, BOLD prayer with the team. She read it to us.

"I pray that on this trip I can hear the voice of God."

I had been praying for Jacqui to know God for years, and so naturally when she asked this specific of a prayer, me of little faith became a little unsure. I have never heard the audible voice of God, and I've been praying for years. I also have enough faith, maybe as much as a mustard seed, to trust God could do a miracle if He chose to do so. I wrote down Jacqui's prayer in my journal. We headed to Uganda.

Going on mission to Redeemer House is one of the most purposeful, fulfilling, and life-changing things I get to do. Redeemer House is our children's home in Uganda that exists to rescue children and work toward reunification with their biological families.

Every trip is special, and every trip is another opportunity to see eyes wide open to who Jesus is and what He can do. Every trip we experience salvation, which is always a miracle! Every trip we get to clothe the naked, feed the hungry, give hope to the hopeless.

We share God's love through acts of service and lifelong friendships we've built with our Ugandan staff, church partners, and sponsor families. Each relationship we share is a miracle. Each meal we share is a miracle. Each time I walk off the plane onto the red dirt roads, it's a miracle. My life as a missionary is a miracle.

I watch the teams we bring experience miracles as well. I have seen the shiest person boldly stand up in a large gathering and share his or her testimony. I have seen young adults hear God's calling on their life and come home to pursue ministry. I have seen people get healed from depression, eating disorders, and back pain. I have seen people surrender their life to Jesus and get baptized. I have seen sick children healed, medical needs met, and youngsters placed in forever families. I have seen drug addicts set free and hopeless people meet Jesus as their Savior. I have seen a five-acre lot of red dirt hills be made into a farm, children's home, guest house, and a place to welcome community for fresh water from the well and living water from God's word. I have seen more miracles than I can count, and I look for them all the time whether here in America or across the world.

We were visiting CSI, Christ Sanctuary International, a church we partner with in Uganda. Pastor Tucker and his wife Pastor Irene served on our board at Redeemer House. They live their lives with such love for God and people. We are always so blessed to stay with them and attend their church.

This particular Sunday, Pastor Tucker finished his sermon in about two hours. We had been in worship for two hours prior to that, and we were wrapping up our four-hour Sunday service when Pastor Tucker closed with an invitation for those who had not yet received God's love and forgiveness to come forward.

He said, "There is a young man in here right now who is here for the first time. You came to CSI to hear about this Jesus we preach, and Jesus wants you to know right now that He has plans for your life and for your children. He wants you to come up here and surrender."

Not even thirty seconds later a young Ugandan man, about twenty-five-years old, wearing a bright yellow soccer jersey, blue jeans, and brown open-toed sandals, put his head down in humility and slowly walked to the front. He knew this was God's prompting. He wanted to surrender. As he lifted his head up to look at Pastor Tucker he began to talk, however, no words came out of his mouth. Pastor Tucker knew immediately this was an example of spiritual warfare. He told the church to sing with him.

He led in worship and prayer, "Chains be broken, Christ is revealed." He sang this over and over, "Chains be broken, Christ is revealed." I could feel the Holy Spirit in a miraculous way. We were all singing as we watched a man who was once lost, now be found. We watched his downcast shame be broken off. We saw his head bowed down and his eyes filled with fear switch to a head looking up and eyes filled with hope. We witnessed as he was unable to speak at the start, but words begin to form once again. We heard him go from silent to praiseworthy. We listened to him pray to Jesus. He was no longer mute...he spoke, and he confessed Jesus as his Lord and Savior. It was a miracle. My entire mission team experienced it.

As we walked back to the guest house from the church, Jacqui was filled with joy. The entire team spoke about what they had just seen. Each telling it from their perspective and what most stood out to them. It reminded me of the gospels, Matthew, Mark, Luke, and John. Each disciple is giving an account of the miracles they saw, yet each is told from a different perspective. This is how it sounded walking back, until Jacqui spoke up and said, "Did you guys hear that thunderstorm? I have never heard thunder like that, and it went on for the entire time of prayer and singing."

The rest of us looked at one another in shock. We were confused. We didn't hear thunder. Not one of the group of eighteen walking back to the guest house, both American missionaries and Ugandan staff, not one heard the thunder. This is when it hit me.

"Jacqui, what was your BIG, BOLD prayer?"

She replied, "To hear God's voice."

I knew it! I knew God's voice in scripture is often compared to thunder. I shared these scriptures with Jacqui. Her eyes filled with tears. Psalm 29:3-4, *"The voice of the Lord is over the waters; The God of glory thunders."* Job 37:4, *"After it a voice roars, He thunders with His majestic voice..."* Psalm 18:13, *"The Lord thundered from heaven, and the most high uttered His voice."* Ezekiel explains God's voice as thunderous, and Revelation describe His voice like thunder. Did God truly just give Jacqui her own private thunderstorm so that she would know He is real?

I believe He did just that. I believe He would answer your BIG, BOLD prayers too if you asked.

9

BROKEN BUT BEAUTIFUL

"Out of his fullness we have all received grace in place of grace already given" (John 1:16).

Spider-Man

In Ethiopia the kids had watched the movie *Spider-Man*. Neb took it to a whole new level. He ran around the compound in search of spiders. Once he caught them, he placed them on his arm and screamed, "Bite me in my blood vein!" As a result of this obsession, Neb knew exactly what he wanted to dress up as when we explained Halloween. He really thought he had superpowers. When he dressed up in that *Spider-Man* costume, his whole world transformed right before our eyes. He made the sounds, shot the silly string out of his hand, and ran up walls.

So many of Neb's "first" experiences left us giggling and laughing. I later asked him if he ever felt as if we were laughing at him. Thankfully, Neb possesses a healthy sense of self-assurance. He understood our laughter resulted from the simple joy of watching him learn and grow.

When the boys introduced Neb to video games, he spent hours in the playroom, as much time as we allowed, playing Marvel superheroes. He didn't care the game was for younger kids. He saw it as the best game ever invented.

Neb played it most often with his youngest brother, at the time. Although Cooper was about six years younger, they meshed well when playing video games. Since Neb was just learning, and Coop was a little guy, they were a pretty even match. Neb always chose to play Spider-Man when given the chance. From outside the playroom, we could hear his sound effects. He loved getting into character from the second the level began and stayed in character all afternoon.

When we started seeing Halloween costumes displayed in stores in early September, Neb, in his learned English, asked us all about Halloween. As we explained, the biggest smile consumed his face at the idea of dressing in a costume, knocking on doors, saying "trick-or-treat" and getting loaded down with candy. What a concept! The whole event amazed him. He sure didn't hesitate to proclaim what costume he'd wear, either.

"Me, Spider-Man!"

I admit, I went a little overboard ordering him an adult-sized Spider-Man costume with all the extra gadgets available. Neb had never worn a costume of any type, so when Spider-Man arrived in the mail in early September, Neb became Spider Man each night until Halloween, and long after October 31. He wore that costume playing the video game. In his mind, it doubled his superpowers and gave him an advantage over his brother.

My heart laughed at the whole idea. It reminded me of toddlers the first time they put on sunglasses and think no one sees them. Or playing hide-and-seek with them and you say, "Ready or not, here I come." Then they say, "I'm over here hiding." They don't quite know all the rules. Instead, they use their imagination to fill in the blanks.

When Cami was two, I took a video of us playing hide-and-seek. I told her to hide, and then I counted. I recorded with my phone as I walked up the stairs. I said, "Cami, here I come."

In the cutest Boston area accent, she replied, "I'm hiding up here, Mom."

No, we are not from Boston, but three of my kids had that accent when they were little. That's a mystery yet to be solved.

On the video, I giggle and say, "Where are you?" I didn't think she would tell me. She did.

"I'm hiding here, Mom, by Daddy's sock drawer. Come find me."

When I followed her voice to her hiding spot, she celebrated, threw her hands up in the air as if signaling a touchdown, and with the loudest giggle, she screams, "I can't believe you found me!" (What is more precious than a child celebrating being found? Oof, and what a spiritual lesson!)

Experiencing all the "firsts" with Neb was such a fun time. None of us, including Neb, knew how to handle all the newness, but we enjoyed every moment. We learned to laugh together and let the little things go. We didn't expect perfection, and we shared so much grace. Like

Cami hiding and being shocked when I found her, Neb put on that costume and then acted surprised when he couldn't perform the real Spider-Man stunts. That didn't stop Sister from hiding or Neb from dressing up. It was all about the fun! Grace upon grace allowed the kids to be kids without expecting them to be someone they were not. Showing them unconditional love and favor, even when they may have deserved a different reaction. It's a shame innocence cannot last a little longer. Enjoy it while you can.

Biracial Struggles Are Real

High school happens to be one place confidence is hard to find. It was all over Twitter, a short clip of my Ethiopian son wearing a Trump shirt while a black girl from his school shot a video of him and wrote, "This brotha confused."

Neb showed me the Tweet and laughed at it. He was not offended, hurt, or angry. He simply thought it was hilarious. He lived in Africa until the age of twelve. If anyone understood the culture of police brutality, injustice, and mob justice, it was Neb. However, there were so many confusing issues all of us had to address becoming a biracial family. We are a beautiful, big, colorful family, and we are so confident God brought us together, even though other people may be confused. We are still assured in our forever family.

We have openly discussed racism in our family. When Neb first arrived, he didn't even know what racism was. He had never been exposed to that in Ethiopia, but our oldest son, Colby, was made aware of the sensitivity of having a black brother very early. In fact, it wasn't Neb who would respond in anger. It was Colby.

I welcomed them back from their soccer tournament at Cherry Island to learn Colby got a red card and was kicked out of the next three games. I was stunned. Colby had never been in a fistfight. He always played aggressively, but I had never seen him lose his temper during a game. I opened my mouth to respond with frustration and reprimand Colby, when Rick calmly motioned me to stop. He said, "Colby did the right thing."

The boys were playing a predominantly white team, opponents they had played against for many years before. Most of the kids knew each other. They had one Hispanic boy and one Asian boy. The remainder of the team was white. That never mattered to us before. In fact, we didn't notice much until we brought home our black son. We were forced to notice.

Neb still didn't speak English very well, but he understood enough to know the comments made to him were not kind. They were personal, not even related to soccer. They fouled him at every opportunity and the other team tag-teamed him, targeting Neb for several reasons. Neb was bigger, faster, and the new kid on the team who scored multiple goals. After the third foul, an opponent player swore at him and said, "You're hella black."

Neb was so confused and replied, "What are you saying? You not white, you brown."

A few plays later, another player ran up behind Neb, kicked his heels and flattened him out. Colby, fed up by this point because the ref ignored the issue, sprinted toward his brother. As he reached Neb lying on the ground, he overheard the opposing player say the n-word. That was it. Without considering the consequences of fighting on the soccer field, Colby started swinging. Neb jumped up and tried to stop the fight, but Colby saw nothing but red. He was ejected from the game immediately.

Because the ref never heard the player antagonize Neb, the other player escaped punishment. I am not one to ever condone violence, but I am one to stand up for what is right and just. Colby did just that. Neb learned something very valuable that day. He discovered his brother would always have his back, no matter the consequence. Neb found unconditional love in our family. He realized we will always stand up for him.

There were a lot of things Neb began understanding about us, and we were learning a lot about him. One of the most challenging things we experienced was hair care. I'm not kidding. Hair care took us some time to figure out.

Rick and I took turns taking Neb to barbers. We learned right away that taking him anywhere except a black barber was a disgrace. Our neighbor, who was from Ghana, told me we should only take him to a black barber. We tried a few, and each time we left discouraged. We didn't realize so many people opposed biracial adoption. This was never something we considered a bad thing. We studied, read books, and took classes, so we knew to be prepared for some opposition, but when we began visiting barbers, it became most evident.

I'll never forget my first trip with Neb. I was the only

one in the shop who looked different, meaning not black. The barbers asked what we wanted done. I showed them a picture Neb had chosen from the internet. They sat Neb in the chair and literally started ripping through his hair with this wide-tooth comb. His head bobbed back and forth, and his eyes watered like a leaking faucet. It was as if they were mad at Neb and appalled by me. I learned, later, they were.

Luckily, Neb didn't know English well enough at the time to understand everything they were saying. But if Neb were their son, they would have shaved his head until he learned to comb it and wear a durag at night.

It was a rough four hours at the barber, and Neb never wanted to return. One of the barbers had some empathy for me. When we were ready to leave, he walked with me down to an ethnic beauty supply story and placed multiple items on the counter for me to buy. He showed Neb what to use and when to use it, and $180 later, we headed home. I'll never forget, after eight weeks passed, I asked Neb if he wanted the same hairstyle. With a very adamant answer, he replied, "Not going back there."

I felt the same way. I thought it was time for Rick to share in the whole hair experience, so I deployed my husband to find a new black barber.

Their experiences at the start were similar. Rick felt uncomfortable, but he was much more confident than I. People could say what they want, and it didn't affect him the same way it affected me. After about three different barbers, Rick finally walked into a little shop off Mack Road and met Barber Tim. This guy has become a family friend and now cuts all my boys' hair. They line up for Barber Tim's "line ups." The thing that made Barber Tim different was his genuine interest in our biracial family. No judgment. No assumptions. Just grace and kindness.

He welcomed us into the culture of his black barber shop as if we belonged there. He learned early on about the details of our adoption, and the work we do in Africa. He has been a huge influence in Neb's life, and we are so grateful for this kind of friendship. Our hope and prayer is to be a "Barber Tim" to those who look different. We will embrace adoption, biracial families, and at-risk youth, and leave the judgment aside. Though adoption can be beautiful, it always starts with brokenness.

Instead of judging, please come alongside and be a part of making the broken beautiful.

Mean Kids Stink

Jason was now nine years old, miraculously healed from possible cerebral palsy. He was walking and talking just like every other little boy in his new school. Jason had his hair cut before our move to Amador County, and in our diverse city of Elk Grove, all Jay ever knew, the haircut was cool. Never had we imagined that being "different" in our new country town would cause such embarrassment and hurt. Jay confidently selected his haircut and had the sides shaved and left the top long enough to braid in a man bun. The haircut happened on a Wednesday night. Thursday morning, he awoke eager to face a new school day.

"Mom, can you please do my man bun?"

"Of course."

I happen to think different is good, and we have embraced his biracial ethnicity and beautiful brown skin. He had confidence, even though he is adopted and looks different from our four biological kids. We did our normal drive to school, enjoyed conversation, music, and a little prayer. When we arrived, he jumped out and headed into his new class.

I proceeded with my day and headed into the office, which was about fifty minutes away from his new elementary school. I got the call at 12:15 p.m. You know, the one. The one every parent wants to avoid.

"Jason is refusing to come back into the class. He is crying and having a fit. I asked him what was wrong, and he said the kids were making fun of his hair. There is nothing we can do to get him back into the class. You'll need to come and get him."

Are you kidding me? I thought. *My son left my car this morning confident, happy. He loved his hair. And now he is an emotional wreck and unable to cope with the onslaught. How on earth am I supposed to handle this?*

Mommy instincts, of course, wanted to race into that classroom and tell those little brat kids exactly what I thought of them. I wanted to be angry. Actually, I *was* angry. Quite angry. I also felt totally helpless. I now had an hour-drive back to school to pick him up. My thoughts swirled like a flushing toilet.

Do I let him cut his hair? Should I have known not to allow him this "different" hair cut? He needs to be tough and not care what others think. It's good to be different, right?

For an hour, I sorted through the emotions and "what

if" scenarios. I had yet to learn what the kids said and who said it, but crying at school and refusing to go back into his classroom meant something triggered the trauma Jason experienced and he was truly undone. He was more than embarrassed. He was hurt. Since I had such a long drive home, I sent Cooper to pick him up immediately. When I arrived home to see Jason on the couch playing Fortnite, my heart was so heavy. I wanted to parent him in a way that would remind him of who he is, who God says he is, and to build up his confidence. I wasn't sure how to do that. I began by asking him to tell me the details. Who? What? Why? When? Where?

"Kids in my class, my whole class, laughed when I walked in. They made fun of my hair at school and on the bus. They called me 'retard,' 'ugly,' 'cat toy,' and 'bun boy.'"

As tears flooded his eyes, I could only embrace him and cry, too. Mean kids stink. I hope it's okay to say that plainly and bluntly, but it is indeed my truth, and maybe even yours. We continue to live and learn. The "man bun" has been put on hold for now.

However, if and when Jay is ready to rock that hair style again, I want him to do it with confidence, knowing his identity comes from within.

10

GROWING TOGETHER

"For this reason, since the day we heard about you, we have not stopped praying for you. We continually ask God to fill you with the knowledge of his will through all the wisdom and understanding that the spirit gives, so that you may live a life worthy of the Lord and please him in every way: bearing fruit in every good work, growing in the knowledge of God" (Colossians 1:9-10).

Pool Party

It took a few moments to realize he was drowning.

His eyes were as big as golf balls peering out of his goggles. I still am not sure what was larger in that moment, Neb's eyes, or the fear he showed. He had told us he could swim.

He assured us multiple times, with the most confident smile and head nod we had seen yet. All our kids learned to swim at a very young age because of the pool in our backyard. On the first warm day of spring, the kids were chomping at the bit. Neb was equally as excited to run and jump in.

"Neb, can you swim?" Rick asked as he moved his arms in the swim motion.

"Yes, Dad, I swim," he replied with confidence.

"Are you sure you swim? Like this?"

Rick again showed him the arm motions of someone swimming. One hand over his head near the ear as he rotated the other over and over as if he himself was swimming. Neb once again confirmed he could swim. He was as sure as sure can be.

The kids jumped in one by one. Cannonballs and big splashes filled the backyard. The giggles and voices escalated. We were in our typical family pool-party mode. Rick and I smiled at each other in relief, knowing Neb could handle himself.

That just made our job of teaching a twelve-year-old to swim so much easier. We sent him off with a little tap on the shoulders. Through the black iron gate, he went. We watched with such anticipation as he was about to experience another "first."

He slipped on his goggles to match the other kids. Then he took a big jump off the diving rock, feet first, into the deepest part of the pool. He kicked his feet and moved his arms in the same swimming motion Rick had shown him, but Neb continued to sink. As his eyes grew in size, we realized something was terribly wrong. He was a fish out of water, the movements were panicked, and he was not at all swimming. Rick and I exchanged panicked looks in pure shock the moment we both realized, "Oh my gosh! He can't swim!"

Before Rick could even pull off his cowboy boots, he dove in the pool to rescue our new son. Fully clothed in jeans and a T-shirt, he dragged Neb from the pool. Astonished, Rick threw his hands in the air, "Neb, you said you could swim?" It was a question more than a statement.

With a nervous smile, Neb replied in his very broken English, thick Ethiopian accent, "Me only swim in lakes." What? Like that cleared up anything.

After about three months of full-time work with Rosetta Stone, Neb was able to communicate more clearly. Once his English was fluent, he was able to clarify the whole swimming/not-swimming episode. Neb thought he knew how to swim. One time at the orphanage, the children took a field trip to a lake. The kids all had the opportunity to "go swimming." That really meant they wore swimming trunks and waded waist deep into the water. It didn't mean they went underwater or jumped in without being able to touch the bottom. It meant they splashed around and played in the lake. Yep. That made sense. Finally.

Throughout the process of learning English, we also tried to communicate with Neb's older sister, Kedija. She went to Dubai for work and sometimes had access to the internet. She would send short video clips talking to us, and used FaceTime whenever she could. I was slightly confused when Neb wouldn't be excited to hear from her. I anticipated a much different response than the disinterested reply he most often displayed. I imagined Neb running to the phone with excitement to talk to his sister, but he didn't. Neb appeared bothered by her calls. It was not until Neb was with us for a couple years, settled in, attached to us, and knew he was staying forever, before he embraced conversations with Kedija.

Like with Neb, communication can sometimes be confusing for all of us. What one person calls swimming, another would call splashing. Learning to communicate with a fluent Amharic child, when no one in the house even knows one word, took patience and creativity. We didn't need to speak the same language to learn to love one another and grow together as a family. Although it was difficult at times, communication continued to improve over time. Boy, what I wouldn't do to have that first pool party on video!

The Donkey and Stories From Neb

We remember being in Kenya on a mission trip and hearing everyone talk about the scar on Neb's forehead. We were told he was kicked in the head by a donkey. The kids at his orphanage, Pastor Buzabi, Pochi, and his sister, Kedija, all shared the same story. Now that Neb is older, he tells this tale differently. He was not just clobbered in the head, he was bucked off that donkey first, then kicked in the head.

When Neb was about six years old, he was riding a donkey. The donkey spooked and began bucking. Neb clung to the donkey for dear life, though he had nothing but the fur to grab. No saddle. No reins. Donkey hair. He thinks he lasted eight seconds, for sure, but in the end, that donkey launched, all four feet in the air, and began bucking so fiercely surely no rodeo pro would survive. Neb tumbled over the side and hit the dirt road. As if to add insult to injury, and more pain, the donkey planted a hoof right to his forehead. To this day, Neb has a perfectly round donkey kick engraved into his forehead.

We laughed as Neb told the tale the way he remembered it.

Neb went on to share other stories, such as how he was always in charge of Titi's goats. Titi was the house mom at Covenant, and she and Neb have always been close. Other than his sister, Kedija, Titi was the one who was in charge of Neb daily. She loved having a strong older boy on-site to help her with the chores that required muscles. He worked the hardest and remembers taking on the role of an older brother seriously. Neb is a natural-born leader. His work ethic and determination make him a force to be reckoned with.

Titi would send Neb and another boy, Tamirat, out in the evenings to watch the goats and sheep. They were in charge of letting them roam in the open field to eat the pasture. Neb and Tamirat's job was to keep them away from Titi's garden. If they had even twenty seconds in the garden, the crops would be demolished. Neb remembers one night when a soccer game was playing at the local village bar—the same bar his dad used to attend. He and Tamirat were instructed to watch the goats and sheep that night. Once they saw them eating in the field, they sneaked over to the bar, peered through the window, watched the game, and returned periodically to check on the flock. The game was close and went overtime with penalty kicks. Neb said time slipped away from them. They were glued to the action on the TV, as if in a trance. They forgot all about the sheep and goats until the game ended. The hour was late. In a panic, they ran back across the field only to find the sheep and goats eating Titi's garden. They thought for sure they were in for a switching, but they managed to catch them just in time to redirect them and save most of the vegetables.

Not only did Titi raise Neb to be a leader at the orphanage, but his teacher at the government school also made him the class leader.

Once his teacher left to get water and put Neb in charge. He handed Neb the long whipping stick and told him, "If one person gets up out of his seat, you must switch him." Neb said it wasn't long before one of the girls from his orphanage, a type of sister to him, got up and wouldn't listen to him. Neb warned her repeatedly, but she refused to sit. With no other choice, he had to switch her and make her sit back down. She gave in after one swat across her legs, but she was not friendly to Neb for days after. Neb told us if he had not done so, and the teacher learned she got up from her seat without punishment, Neb would have been badly switched. Neb didn't mind being the man in charge, but he didn't enjoy handing out discipline. He always did what was necessary to avoid being punished.

Natural-Born Leaders

Whether Neb was in his classroom directing the younger

children, or helping with sheep, he was called to leadership. We saw this quality in Neb the week we met him at Covenant. He was absolutely in charge, and the other children knew it. When it came time to pick soccer teams, he was one of the captains. One of our favorite memories from when we went there to bring him home was watching Neb, his friends, and our oldest son, Colby, play soccer for hours in the field. Neb and Colby were on the same team each time, and they played against groups of boys. We brought soccer jerseys on that trip which were donated from the Elk Grove Youth Soccer League. Watching their glee amidst all the turmoil added fuel to our resolve.

Colby is a leader too, and he had the idea to host a soccer jersey drive. Once he knew he would be traveling with us to Ethiopia to pick up his brother, he wanted to gather as many soccer jerseys as possible. He wanted to deliver soccer jerseys to the kids in the village and to all Neb's friends. Our soccer community in Elk Grove, CA, came alongside us in such exemplary ways. The league board invited Colby to speak at a coaches meeting where he shared his idea with over seventy local coaches. It was such a proud moment for Rick and me, and that was the start of our first soccer jersey drive. That drive collected over four-hundred jerseys. Each year after the jersey drive grew larger and larger. We began collecting jerseys, cleats, and balls. We use that equipment annually on our mission trips, and we even had the opportunity to take additional players from the soccer league and host soccer clinics in Uganda. These jerseys have been a catalyst for us to provide clothing and share the love of God with thousands of children.

Colby and Neb took turns scoring goals. They were both equally competitive, and the village team of kids kept growing bigger and bigger. We started with a pickup game of about twelve children, six vs. six, and they were all from the orphanage. As the village children began to hear the kids playing, they came flying in like it was a circus act. One by one, the teams grew and grew. It took about twenty kids to finally score on Neb and Colby. After watching the boys play for several hours, we knew Neb was going to fit right in. Colby's soccer team at home was going to be very impressed. We were bringing home another competitive soccer player.

11

FIGHT THE GOOD FIGHT

*"Let perseverance finish its work so that you may be mature
and complete, not lacking anything"* (James 1:4).

TKO—Technical Knockout

Training is not easy. It takes endurance, hard work, and
sometimes even a TKO. As parents, we should train our
children in the way they should go. This doesn't sound too
hard. Training for a boxing match seems more difficult.
However, when the TKOs become a reality in parenting,
injury to your physical body is nothing compared to the
emotional and spiritual sadness that threatens to take
over. Parents want their children to grow up and be amazing human beings. We want children who do good, work
hard, and contribute to society and the lives of others.
We want to know we raised good kids. When the rubber
meets the road, we can do our part and still experience the
pain of older children making poor choices. We can get
in the ring with them over and over and still leave just as
beat up as the time before. We can train our children, but

we cannot control them. We can discipline them, but we cannot always stop them from making horrible mistakes.

When Neb was a teenager, he became very disrespectful towards me. He wouldn't talk back to his dad, but he had no problem treating me as if I was an annoying younger sister. Training him up during this time was an unending cycle. It seemed repetitive and impossible. Once, when Neb rebelled, he talked back to me in front of my husband, his dad. Despite gentle warnings, he continued his abrupt, disrespectful approach. While it's easy to understand, much of his behavior likely resulted from changing teenage hormones, that was no excuse. Rick would not allow him to treat me with such disrespect.

Continuing his teenage tantrum, Neb snatched the groceries from my hands and gave me a defiant look. That was it. Rick reached to grab hold of Neb's arm to stop him in his tracks and redirect his course. This movement triggered a fear within, and he bolted. He ran out of our garage and down the street.

Oh my gosh! He's running away in his boxers! That was my first thought. At least, I am pretty sure I didn't say it aloud.

Neb ran barefoot in his boxers. Yep, he ran, unclothed, clad only in his boxers.

Rick must have seen my face change from the shock of Neb's sudden bolting, to eyes wide open, realizing his state of dress, to fear that my son was running away.

"He'll be back," Rick said, his voice low and calm. But as the seconds passed his image became smaller and smaller with the distance. We stood there, waiting for him to turn and look back. He didn't. He just kept running. It was then we both realized he had no intention of coming back. Each time we yelled his name louder, the harder and faster he ran.

At the time, we lived in a bedroom community neighborhood in Elk Grove, CA. Outside the entrance of our neighborhood were busy city streets lined with popular stores, national chains, restaurants, and more. Hour by hour passed, and the sun dropped closer to the horizon. Rick remained unworried. He believed Neb would come back. On the other hand, I was in full-mode panic. I imagined a police helicopter circling our neighborhood. I could almost hear a repetitive announcement coming across the loudspeaker, "Lost Ethiopian boy, age fourteen, wearing only boxers. Please call 9-1-1 if you see him."

The fear took over. We needed a search party. We gathered a few neighbors and friends and departed in small groups, looking in different directions. Some walked down a nearby nature preserve trail. Some headed east to the creek. A few jumped in their cars and drove all around the outside of the neighborhood.

Still, Rick assumed Neb hid somewhere nearby, mostly likely in a bush, watching us all scurry around looking for him. After all, how could he go far in just his bare feet and boxers?

Thirty more minutes passed. We contemplated calling the police. We sent a prayer request to our best friends who lived across town, exactly 3.6 miles from us, alerting them that Neb had run away in his boxers. Being such devoted friends who parented alongside us for over a decade, through all kinds of joys and trials, we knew they would pray. Of course, they did much more than that. Their oldest daughter, Molly, decided to walk and look for Neb in case he ran to some place familiar.

Maybe she had a hunch. Maybe she knew Neb well enough to guess where he might be. Maybe she put herself in his shoes to figure out where he might go.

Neb stayed overnight hundreds of times at the Harrison home with his friend Jeffrey. His high school was also within walking distance from the Harrison's. As Molly walked, she spotted an Ethiopian fourteen-year-old boy in his boxers.

"Molly, I need some clothes. Can you sneak me in Jeffrey's window?"

Sneaking in windows? Nope. Instead, Molly convinced Neb to enter through the front door and let her parents talk to him. She assured Neb he was safe and informed him we were worried sick and had been searching for him.

Neb trusted Molly and spent the next couple of hours in counseling with our best friends. Of course, they had immediately texted us he was safe, but asked us not to come over until they talked with him.

Neb needed a safe place. He knew where to find one. Kids need a safe place outside their own homes, at times. This episode proved that none of us can or should try to parent our children alone. We wanted our kids to have adults in their lives who they feel safe to "run to" when they don't trust Mom or Dad will understand. Raising a family does take a village, and we are so thankful for ours.

Running Away

I wish I could say that was the only time Neb ran away. It wasn't. We reconciled and moved forward, but back into the ring we went when he turned eighteen. Throughout his teen years, Neb became a bit arrogant. When he turned eighteen, he assumed he could do life on his own. What eighteen-year-old doesn't think, since they've finally become an adult, they've got it all figured out? They assume, since they are a full-fledged adult, they can do what they want, right?

Neb was an adult, but he still lived in our home, we expected him to follow the rules we set. One point of contention was the boundaries and expectations we established for cell phones. We created parental restrictions when they were younger, and as they matured, and could be trusted, we gave them more and more freedom with their phones. However, there are things, regardless of their age, we will not allow in our home: explicit music, porn, and inappropriate X-rated shows/websites. We have littles following in the footsteps of our older kids, and we expect them to set good examples. We also believe there are spiritual repercussions that come with some types of media. In the training of raising children, this is one of the most difficult areas we have parented. We are still trying to figure it all out. Things that seem so normal to the world are off limits in our home. And so, into the boxing ring we went, again.

One Saturday night, I read something on Neb's social media that was offensive and inappropriate. He didn't write it, but he shared it. I went downstairs calmly, to talk to him about the post. Neb was not in the mood. I'm an extrovert, and he is an introvert. It took us years to relate to one another in that regard. The moment Neb decided he was done talking, there was nothing I could do. I learned this the hard way whenever I tried to force him to talk. It never worked. He is strong-willed, determined, and he decided when the right time was for him. We would let him go to his room with no media and pray. (Well, we hoped that's what he was doing.) We grounded him until he was ready to talk. Sometimes it took Neb thirty minutes, and sometimes it took three days. We waited patiently. When he was ready, we would talk.

This was one of those times. Neb wasn't ready to talk about the social media post. So I simply said, "You have until tomorrow morning before church to remove that post, or you will lose your phone." I walked out of his room. I felt like we could have discussed it. I could have explained why it was inappropriate. However, Neb didn't want to talk. Neb did not expect us to remove the phone without a discussion.

Morning came. Rick's responsibilities as an elder required that he arrive earlier, so he had already left for church. As we were preparing to go to service, I noticed Neb hadn't removed the post. I put out my hand as he walked by.

"Hand me your phone. It is now mine."

"What? You can't take my phone. If you don't like my social media, unfollow me. I didn't ask you to look at my posts anyway."

He walked by me with his phone so tightly gripped in his hands there was no way for me to physically remove it. His reply and attitude shocked me. *Ugh. Into the boxing ring we go, again.*

I prayed quietly, then followed him down the hall. I repeated myself with more authority in my voice, "Neb, hand me the phone now. I told you last night what I expected. You have had time to obey."

Throwing the phone toward me, he stomped off to his room.

"I hate you. I am not going to church."

I seethed. How dare he speak to me that way and be so hateful. By the time I arrived at church, I was totally irate. I was downright angry. I was so mad at that "entitled brat" I could hardly handle myself. By the time I stepped into the building, Rick already knew there had been an episode at home. Neb called Rick using Wi-Fi on his old iPod. Grrrr!

Neb always figured out how to get what he needed. He was a survivor, after all. Although that trait can be incredibly helpful in life, it doesn't feel helpful to the parent who is fighting for a child. I wondered what Neb had said to Rick. I was still mad.

Deep breath in. Deep breath out.

Then the worship music began to play, and I knew I needed nothing more than to be in the presence of Jesus. There. Peace began to seep in. It was one of those divine moments I could see clearly how God's grace is sufficient.

After church, Rick told me Neb was leaving. He was packing his stuff. He was moving out. He would be gone when we got back. I was shocked. I was speechless.

I asked Rick question after question. I talked a mile a minute. Fear took over, again. "Where would he go? How would he live on his own? What is he taking? What should we do? Will he survive?" I should have known. Neb had been ready to figure out life on his own for a while, and his attitude toward authority revealed it. Everything had been building up to this moment. The more I stepped into the ring with Neb, the more rebellious he became. There were things Neb wanted to do, and nothing we said or did could change his ways. He knew right from wrong, and he knew what the Bible commanded. He just didn't care.

I didn't sleep the first night. Sadness kept me awake. My mind refused to shut down. I questioned all I said and did and cried most of the night. I prayed for his safety, and I was devastated. I did not know where he was. I am glad I didn't know; because I later learned he tried to sleep in his car in the Wal-Mart parking lot. That is just not safe! Thankfully, we had friends who intercepted him, and I was not mad about it. I believe I worried for a reason. I prayed away the worry the only way I knew how, and Neb stayed away from us for a little less than two weeks. It was awful. I cried daily, even though I knew we had to wait for his return. In the meantime, Rick had talked to Neb and had given him two options. One, he could come back and talk through the incident with us. Or two, he had twenty-four hours to take over all the adult responsibilities that accompany adulting. This meant he needed to come to our home, and pick up the signed title to his car, get a new cell phone plan in his name, and pack up anything left in his room he wanted to keep.

Rick let him know if he didn't do that, the car would be considered stolen and all other five siblings had dibs on his room and belongings. Neb, still not ready to talk, chose option two. He stopped by that evening, picked up the title we signed. He grabbed a few more things from his room, including his pillow and comforter, and he went to get a cell phone in his name. I learned he had been staying on the couch at my sister-in-law and brother-in-law's house. It hurt me the first time I drove by their house. They lived around the corner. I drove by multiple times a day. My heart broken seeing Neb's car parked outside their home. I waited three days before I called my sister-in-law, Angelica, to ask some questions. Remember how I said, "It takes a village?" Well, it does, but when there is a broken relationship between parents and child, the last thing a parent wants is for other adults to influence them in ways that cause more division.

I knew better than that fear, but I also knew if I didn't ask Angelica some questions and have a hard conversation, she might not know exactly what had happened. We chatted in detail. She explained that her daughter, Taylynn, had learned Neb planned to sleep in the Wal-Mart parking lot, so she invited him to stay temporarily at their house instead. Angelica helped Neb figure out how to register his car, how to request insurance quotes, and walked him through selecting the best insurance. She talked to me daily, and we agreed it best to give Neb space. After a "cool off" period, she and her husband would sit with Neb and discuss forgiveness and reconciliation. We all knew this scenario could easily cause division, and we needed to be careful.

After Neb spent about nine days in the other Cross home, we finally scheduled a family meeting. Neb shared some hurts with Angelica and Will he had never told us. Neb was triggered by my response to the social media, mostly because he didn't like being told what to do, but his response came from deeper issues. I was so humbled when we sat together, and he reminded me of two things I said to him in years past that hurt him. I didn't even remember blaming Neb for a disagreement Rick and I had. But I believed Neb when he said I looked him in the face during this fight and said, "This is all your fault. You did this."

He also reminded me once when Rick disciplined him several years prior, I made the comment, "You walked away like a scared dog."

These are a few of the most humbling details I can share with you. When he repeated what I had said in my anger, I was mortified. I was shocked at myself to have said such things to him, but clearly, he hadn't made it up. My words pierced the deepest part of him, and he couldn't move past it. This is why the Bible instructs us to be slow to anger and quick to listen. Our words damage people, and kids who come from trauma are triggered by some of these words in ways we could never comprehend.

Obviously, I apologized to Neb for the things I said that hurt him. We talked in more detail about what it looked like as an adult to live in our home, and regardless of age, there would be honor and respect.

Our rules regarding biblical truths did not change because our kids turned eighteen. In our home, those biblical truths applied to even the adults. We prayed together and gave God thanks, once again, for the village that supports our family. It was helpful for Neb to have his auntie and uncle by his side, and we trusted them to be the mediators. It was a beautiful night of reconciliation, and it started us on the road to healing.

Being knocked out doesn't mean we stay down in the ring. It means we need to recover and work at being ready once again. In this scenario, we invited Neb to move back home, and we gave him a couple contracts to look over. The contracts we made created boundaries and gave him some options. He could pay us rent and live there as a "roommate," still adhering to the obvious rules of no drugs, alcohol, girls sleeping over, etc. Or he could live there without paying rent in the family model and take part in chores, family dinners, church, and helping with the younger kids.

He looked over those contracts for twenty-four hours, and he came back with the family model signed. He moved back into his room flawlessly. I mean, some of his clothes were located in his brothers' dressers, but they graciously returned it all. We celebrated Neb's homecoming, and we embraced the next couple years with him before he launched out into adult life as a married, mature, hard-working, Jesus-loving young man!

12

OUR MESS IS ALSO
OUR MESSAGE

"There is no fear in love. But perfect love drives out fear, because fear has to do with punishment. The one who fears is not made perfect in love" (1 John 4:18).

Fearful Triggers

I was dying. I drove myself to the doctor's office in severe pain. I contemplated calling my family and friends and saying my goodbyes. The pain in my head was so excruciating, I convinced myself I had a brain aneurysm. I'm not one to get headaches, I do not have a history of migraines, and I never had a sinus infection. This pain came on so suddenly and was so brutal. I knew I was dying.

I called my sister-in-law, who is also my best friend. She was graciously babysitting three of my children at the time.

"Angelica, I am on my way to the doctor's office, but I am sure I am dying. This is more pain than I can handle. Please make sure my kids know how much I love them.

Help Rick when I am gone." Even in my dying declaration, she never skipped a beat.

"My goodness, you are not. You are going to be fine. Let me pray for you ..." And she did.

Having a tribe of friends who cover you in prayer is the best gift anyone can ask for. When you come to a place in life when you frantically or fearfully call a friend, and instead of giving you their advice, they reply with, "Let me pray with you," keep that friend. Put that friend on speed dial. Nothing casts out fear, calms anger, or restores you to a place of peace better than someone immediately praying for you. I've reached a place in my life now that if someone says to me, "I'll be praying for you," I often say, "Can you pray for me now?" Be a prayer warrior for those around you, and hope they also pray for you. Prayer changes everything!

After I talked to Angelica, I called my mom. I told her I was on my way into the doctor's office, and I could be dying. Yep. Terrible idea. Bless her heart. I worried her in a way no mom should ever worry. I should have known better, but I truly believed I was nearing my end. I needed her to know how much I loved, valued, and honored her. My mom truly is one of God's greatest gifts. She is full of unconditional love for everyone. She lives her life daily on high alert and asks God each morning, "To whom can I be blessing today?" I want to be just like her when I grow up.

What a way to meet a new doctor. The waiting room was small, with a few chairs and a coffee table with magazines. When I approached the counter to check in, a young and vibrant receptionist greeted me with such enthusiasm I almost forgot where I was. I handed her my medical card, paid my deductible, and took a seat in the waiting area. About fifteen minutes later, a medical assistant, dressed in lavender scrubs with flower print, called my name. She weighed me, measured my height, and escorted me into Room 3. She sat down and began to ask questions.

"So, Mrs. Cross, what brings you in today?"

"I am having a brain aneurysm."

"Okay, rewind, did someone tell you that?"

"No, my mom's friend had one a few years back, and she passed away. It started with a really painful headache and Tylenol or Motrin wouldn't help at all. That's exactly what is happening to me. The pain just keeps getting worse and worse, and I can't even lay my head on the pillow."

"When did this head pain begin?"

"Three days ago, and each day it gets more and more painful."

"Any other symptoms, Mrs. Cross?"

"If I have any other symptoms, I can't tell because my head hurts too bad to even think about anything else."

She typed all this information on the computer, took my blood pressure, handed me a hospital gown, and instructed me to undress. She reminded me to leave the opening of the gown in the back. Before she left the room, she said the doctor would be right in. I waited, and I prayed. I convinced myself the doctor would take one look at me and rush me straight to the hospital by ambulance.

"Hello, Mrs. Cross. I understand you have severe head pain. Let's take a look at what's going on."

The doctor, a little 5'4" gray-haired lady, set the earpieces of her stethoscope in place, picked up the chest piece, placed the cold metal against my skin and listened.

"Deep breath in … and out."

After listening for a few seconds, repeating the process, she asked me about congestion, cough, allergies, etc. She looked in my ears and pressed down on some pressure points. In the most matter-of-fact tone, she said, "Well it looks like you have a very painful sinus infection going on. I am going to call in an antibiotic, and after forty-eight hours you are going to feel so much better. The pressure will end, but even after you feel better, continue taking the antibiotics for the remaining twelve days."

What? I'm not dying? Are you sure?

The shock turned to a few happy tears, but only after I asked her several times, "Are you sure it's just a sinus infection?"

I had convinced myself it was the end, but it was a sinus infection. Have you ever had one? Oh. My. Goodness. I have real empathy now for anyone suffering from a sinus infection. In the past, I never thought much about it, but experiencing it for myself, now I know the pain someone suffers from it.

Do It Afraid

I spend the day with our first grandbaby, baby Cash, on Fun Fridays. However, one particular Fun Friday took a terrible U-turn when I received a call from Jason's school nurse around mid-morning. Jason was suffering severe tooth pain.

Although adoption is beautiful, it comes from real broken places of hardship and pain. Both physical pain and emotional pain are the results of children growing up in adoptive families. The loss is impossible to reconcile, but hope and love abide deeply. Because alcohol and methamphetamines were used in utero, Jason struggled immensely with tooth damage. As his tiny baby teeth grew in, we learned he had a disorder which caused the enamel to erode. We found ourselves praying earnestly for his adult teeth to come in more strongly than his baby teeth. Constant grinding during his sleep as a young baby, Jason's teeth had been worn nearly to his gums. The nerves were exposed, and the pain created enough discomfort Jason cried all the way from our small town of Sutter Creek to our dentist in Elk Grove. The fifty-minute drive was excruciating for both of us. My heart broke for him as he covered his right cheek with his hand and a waterfall of gator tears fell from his eyes. I knew the pain was intense. I just didn't foresee what we were about to endure.

Cash's eyeballs were the size of golf balls as he peered at his ten-year-old Uncle Jay's squirming and squealing for help. Because our Fun Friday took a turn for the worse, I figured my ten-month-old grandson could endure the emergency dentist appointment without being traumatized. However, Cash wasn't the one having a hard time. It was me. As Jason lay on that dental chair in complete terror, the dentist gave the diagnosis and treatment plan. Jason needed two emergency extractions. Fear took root right away, far deeper than the two teeth that needed to be removed.

I reached deep for my best calming voice and coached Jason. I tried to be his biggest fan, "You can do it. It's numb you won't feel it. Be a big boy. Baby Cash is watching ..."

When the dentist touched his cheek, he squealed for help. This beautiful pediatric dentist office, specializing in kid-friendly staff and relaxing environment, had just met its match. An office made of brightly painted rainbows and balloons, a place known to make going to a children's dentist office fun and enjoyable, now emitted the sound of a haunted house, all coming from our ten-year-old son.

Gut-hurling screams echoed throughout. "Help, you're killing me!"

I think Jason believed it, too.

My armpits began to sweat. Red hives formed all over my chest. My grandson seemed to weigh a hundred pounds. My nerves caught fire, burning hot with panic. My mind followed.

What if he won't calm down? What am I to do? Of course, I did the only thing I knew to do in times of severe panic. I prayed. There was no instant relief. Next?

I tried to encourage Jason by saying all the most calming things that came to mind. Over the squeals and screams, I instructed Jay to pray. He couldn't hear me or chose not to listen. He was one hundred percent operating out of fear, and it was as if he were deaf. Not one word from my mouth felt encouraging to him. I breathed in and counted to three, then realized the only person with any hope to talk him off the ledge was my husband. Rick stands a full 6'6" and is the biggest presence in our lives. I tried FaceTime. He didn't answer. I took a breath, again, and counted to three. I called back. For Rick and I, a repeated call is our emergency signal. We know if we receive one, we need to step away from whatever we are doing to take the call. The third time was the charm. Rick answered, clearly panicked because he knew I needed him to walk away from a meeting. I looked him in the eyes, but before I utter a word he asked, "Dang it, babe, is someone dying?"

In exasperated panic, I said, "No, not really, but Jason thinks he is dying, so it seems one and the same in the moment? I need your help." I explained the situation and Rick stepped in to do what he does best. He talked to Jay with kindness and patience.

"It's okay to be afraid. It will be uncomfortable for a short time. As soon as the dentist does his job, the pain will be gone, and the healing process begins."

Jason began to listen and wipe away some tears. Rick continued. "Jason, Daddy will be right here on the phone watching every move the dentist makes. I'll be right here watching you be self-controlled and brave. I'll be right here until the very end. You are strong. You are brave. I am with you. I know you can do it, buddy."

To be honest, Jason was still afraid, but our children have heard us say multiple times in our own lives, "I will do it afraid."

In this very scary situation, Rick expected Jason to do it afraid. It reminds me of what Jesus does for us when He allows us to go through the trials of this world, calls us into the mission field, asks us to say yes to adoption, sends us to new places or a new career, and positions us to stand with others during loss and grief, He is expecting us to do it afraid. Like Jesus, we stand with our children, we cheer them on, and we expect them to believe that they can do all things through Christ who gives them strength.

Jason took in three big breaths, closed his eyes, and with courage said to the dentist, "OKAY, GO!"

The dentist looked at me and asked, "If I get a grip on the tooth, do you want me to pull it no matter what his reaction is?" This was take three. I was not about to walk out of that place with unfinished business. The hard part was done. The four shots of sleepy juice were administered. Jason was fully numb.

I gave the nod.

"You pull those teeth no matter what."

I knew Jason was not in pain, but he associated the pulling with pain. I knew once those teeth were removed, the nerves would no longer cause him severe pain. We knew as his parents this was the best thing for him and it needed to be done. Jason's reaction to having his two teeth pulled is the same reaction many of us have when God calls us to do something new, and perhaps scary. We may kick and scream. We may feel as though we are dying. We may have to try three or four times. The good news about trusting our Heavenly Father is that when we do it afraid, He stands with us until we get to the other side. He brings to life the rainbows on the wall as we walk out of the dentist office differently. No more pain. No more fear. No more kicking and screaming. Fear is replaced with peace and pain is replaced with tranquility. It was a testament to the perseverance of faith. Baby Cash witnessed one of God's miracles that day, and hopefully many more to come.

Tears Can Heal

When Neb was a senior in high school, he had his first "girlfriend." We encouraged our boys to wait until they were older to date. We wanted them to date for marriage and not for fun. It hurts me to know some young men will try out girls like some people test-drive vehicles. Our family values purity and God's instruction on marriage, so we began those conversations early. The conversations were not a bullet-proof guarantee our kids would obey God's word; however, we taught it in faith.

When Neb began to date his very good friend, I must be honest, I was a bit nervous. I was anxious because they didn't share all the same values. I didn't see it being a relationship that would lead to marriage. I was concerned. After talking with Neb about it, he still decided to give it a "try." We embraced this short relationship, and then she broke his heart. I mean, she really did break his heart. He was not expecting someone to leave him again. The break-up triggered loss, trauma, abandonment, and grief Neb had not yet processed from childhood. The night she communicated to him her desire to only be friends, he broke down. It was a hard evening. However, eventually, his breaking turned into a good thing. I've heard it said, "God makes the broken beautiful." In this situation God did just that, but it didn't come without hard conversations, prayer, and worship music playing unapologetically in the background.

I hadn't seen Neb cry since we had adopted him. In six

years, I hadn't witnessed him shed a single tear. He had never talked to me about his biological mom. When his heart was freshly wounded from this breakup, I sat on the floor next to his bed. I brushed my hand up and down his arm while I silently prayed for God's wisdom and peace. I asked God to give me words to encourage him. I asked God to speak through me. I prayed for God to use me to remind Neb of God's never-ending and unconditional love. I prayed and prayed, and finally I had the words to initiate the most intimate conversation I've ever had with my seventeen-year-old son. It was the conversation I had always hoped and prayed for. However, Neb was twelve when we adopted him. I didn't know if we would ever grow to this place. It was a moment in our relationship I will never forget. I call it a breakthrough and continue to celebrate it to this very today.

Four hours in his room together talking, crying, praying, and singing felt like four minutes. The time flew by as we settled into precious territory together. While it was mine and Neb's first breakthrough conversation, it was not our last. Thankfully, Neb and I now have a relationship that leads us into precious territory regularly. We go to deep places in our faith, our decisions, our convictions, our failures, and our futures together. We sharpen one another, and it's a precious gift for a mom.

Through his tears Neb said, "I didn't even grieve. I didn't shed a tear when my mom died. All I remember is everyone in the tiny house huddled together, weeping and moaning, and me running outside to play. I would look in the door, and they would still be crying. I didn't even cry when my mom died."

Neb was under three years old when his mom died, but he believed a lie from that day. He believed he should have been mature enough to properly grieve. He believed he should have cried just like his older sister, and like his mom's friends from the village. He felt guilt and shame for crying over a girl he briefly dated, but he didn't shed a tear when his mom died. This was a real trigger for Neb, and we had to talk through it. We needed scriptures, prayer, and the promises of God to lead Neb to healing in the deepest places.

For many, it might be easy to wave this off, and tell Neb, he was just a baby, with no foundation to know any better. However, sometimes the enemy uses simple lies and plants them deep within. These lies become a foothold we start to believe, and the next thing you know, we grow up feeling shame and guilt rather than walking in freedom.

Squeaky Wheel

Shame is a lie that can follow us from childhood. As a child I believed the lie that I was like a squeaky wheel. No one said this to me, my parents never made me feel that way, and I have no idea why I clung to that lie, but I did. I am a verbal processer. I feel most significant with a microphone in my hand. I want to be heard. Believing communication is one of my strengths makes sense now, but early in my life I believed I was an annoying squeaky wheel that wouldn't stop making noise. I felt self-conscious and forced myself to be careful not to talk too much.

I recently went to the writing retreat at The Oaks Center led by Bob Goff. Rolling into this retreat in a borrowed, white 2008 Lexus, I prepared to learn all about the writing process. I wanted to soak it all in, like a sponge. As I was driving through the gorgeous views into the retreat center, I rolled my window down. This is when I realized the car my mom's friend loaned me to drive from the San Diego airport to Romana had a very squeaky wheel. The quiet serene ambiance of the beautiful green pastures, horses galloping in the distance, and birds chirping, were all overcome by a loud and obnoxious squeaky wheel. I felt embarrassed as I pulled up and was greeted by the welcome team. There was no way they missed that noise, but they thrive on Southern hospitality. They ignored the noise and welcomed me with enthusiasm.

On day two of the retreat, I felt motivated, encouraged, and more inspired to write a book than ever before. Kimberly and Bob taught a session on creating a sizzle reel. I took notes and had a few questions. When Kimberly walked back into the cabin around 10 that night, after a super long day, I cornered her.

"Kimberly, I know you are really tired, but tomorrow can we sit down and chat more about the squeaky wheel?"

"The what?"

In complete confusion, the look on her face said it all. I realized I said, "squeaky wheel," and that is not what a thirty-second film of me speaking publicly is called. A sizzle reel is what I meant to say. I had such insecurities rise after listening to Bob and Kimberly encourage us to create a "sizzle reel," small clips of us speaking, similar to a quick highlight reel to share these clips with audiences and organizations who would benefit from hearing us share. To me, this meant moms' groups, women's groups, foster/adopt groups, churches, and mission agencies or teams. I had been asked to speak several times in the past, and each time was as exciting as the last. I am always so honored, and it is an easy yes for me when I am invited anywhere. There are audiences that I have always hoped to speak to, but inviting myself by sending a sizzle reel took me back to believing that lie. I thought of myself as a squeaky wheel no one wanted to hear.

It was Bob Goff who looked at me and said, "You have so much to share. Go write your book. People need to hear all about it."

Kimberly chimed in, "You talk about going to Africa like it's something people do all the time. You have stories to share. Go do it. You would be such an encouragement to young moms who have little kids since you have been there and done that."

Bob and Kimberly motivated me enough to become ten times bolder in letting the world know I enjoy being an encouragement to others, and I would be open to speaking at their events. What an honor and joy it is to be given this opportunity. I now give thanks to God for creating in me the gift of communication. What was once something that caused me great insecurity is now one of my greatest honors.

In the same way, Neb had a hard time receiving all the

love we were showing him because he didn't feel like he deserved it. He wanted to celebrate the beautiful home we lived in, the abundant food choices, the plethora of clothes, and shoes he was given. However, he felt guilt about those provisions. He knew there were kids on the streets, kids in the orphanage, and children like him who had nothing. There is healing and work to be done for all young ones who experience trauma, and sometimes we want to relate, but we just can't.

This is why, when Neb returned from Ethiopia in 2018 and changed his major from construction management to social work, I rejoiced with such affirmation. Neb said, "I want to help kids like me." He is doing just that, and I believe it is only the start. I dream of the days he can visit with adopted children and talk to them openly about the trauma and the hope for healing. I dream of the day when he places a foster care child in a forever family. I dream of the day he will walk with that child through the transition, relate to the feelings of insecurity, sadness, and help them learn to receive love and provision without guilt and shame. I dream of the day Neb can use his "mess" as a "message" to kids just like him.

13

GIFTS

"Every good and perfect gift comes from above" (James 1:17).

Promise Ring

Rick gave me a promise ring when we first met. He said from the very start he was going to marry me. He was sure of it. I hadn't yet given in to the idea. I'll be the first to admit, I think the promise ring meant more to Rick than it did to me. I didn't know this until I passed that ring to Nebeyu's sister, Kedija.

It wasn't planned. I didn't wear that diamond ring to Ethiopia to give it away. I wore that ring because it was a small diamond without much monetary value. Before we traveled, they advised us to avoid wearing large diamonds or anything that would draw attention to any riches. The little promise ring stuffed away in the top drawer of my jewelry box seemed the perfect solution.

Kedija was only thirteen years old when her mother passed away. In American culture, most thirteen-year-old children spend their time occupied with things like hobbies, learning to play piano, playing competitive soccer, attending youth groups, and participating in middle school dances. In Africa at thirteen, most young girls are doing things we consider mommy duties. These little ladies discover how to cook with fire and with hot coal as young as four years old. As soon as they can walk, they learn where to gather water and how to carry it on their heads for the miles-long treks back to their huts. They understand to wash laundry in streams or puddles, cut vegetables with makeshift knives, and tend to the garden. Life for Kedija was all this and more. She not only assumed the role of cooking and providing for Neb, but she shouldered the responsibility of protecting him from their new abusive stepmom.

As mentioned earlier, Neb's father was a Muslim man with many wives. Neb's mom was the last wife he took, and Muhammad treasured her. She gave birth to Kedija, Tigist, and Neb, Muhammad's youngest three children. When she passed away, the natural thing to do for Muhammad was to combine families. He brought one of his other wives and his other children into the home where Neb and Kedija lived before their mother died. This forced Kedija to grow up even more quickly than culturally expected. For three years Kedija protected, provided for, and lived her life as Neb's mother figure. I know he didn't like it then, but looking back, he appreciated it. Tigist was sent to the capital of Ethiopia, Adis Abiba, to live with extended family and attend school. It was Kedija's idea for Neb to be enrolled at the orphanage. She knew the possibility he may be adopted, and she might never see him again. She embraced the difficulty of sacrificial love because she knew it would be best for Neb. She did whatever it took to make that happen.

When we met Kedija on our trip to pick up Neb, my heart broke. She was sixteen years old at the time and a servant in Dubai. She made a most difficult choice of signing away her rights and giving them over to a family in Dubai with a promise to have a safe home, food, and work. Only by the grace of God was Kedija able to leave Dubai and return to Ethiopia to send her little brother off to his new family. She needed to meet us. She had to know her little brother was joining a family who loved him. Our joy of adoption offered fairytale-like feelings. My heart ached watching Kedija wrestle between the painful heartbreak and the beauty of adoption. I felt her sorrow as she hugged him. She didn't want to leave his side, and although it was irritating to Neb, she was struggling with this goodbye. Would she ever see him again? Would he be safe? Would we protect him and provide for him as she had done all these years? She worried the way a mother worries.

The night before we left, during our final time of prayer, worship, and goodbyes, reality set in. Kedija would be leaving her brother that night for the last time. She would hug him and tell him goodnight for the last time. While in the back of the room, as we were cutting up an onion for our meal, I looked up to see Kedija watching Neb from afar. She caught me staring at her, and with strained, broken English she said, "Mama, you promise to take my brother? You promise care for him? Cooking? School?"

I looked down at the promise ring on my hand. I stood from the upside-down bucket, also known as my cooking stool. With no thought at all, as if superpowers took over, I pulled off the ring. I looked her in the eyes and said, "Kedija, I promise to be the best mom to Neb that I can be. I promise to love him and protect him. I promise to train him up in the word of God. I promise to send him to school and to cook for him. I promise, Kedija, that we love him already, and we will always love him."

I removed the ring that had once been a token of Rick's promise to me and placed it on Kedija's finger. I held her close. Her tears drenched my xHope t-shirt, but I didn't mind. My tears, too, wet her shoulder as we embraced.

I do not like to make promises. I will usually avoid a promise at all costs. I prefer to say that I will try, or I will do my best, but in adopting our son Neb, I knew those were promises I could make. I understood this because they were the same promises God made to me, and He fulfilled them all.

Nebeyu Means Prophet

Having the gift of prophecy is not the same as being a fortune teller. When people think of prophecy, they often think of telling the future. Mark Batterson says it best in *The Grave Robber*, "Prophet means someone who speaks words of strength, comfort, and encouragement inspired by the Holy Spirit."[1] When Neb was born, his

---

1 Batterson, Mark, and Parker Batterson. The Grave Robber: How Jesus Can Make Your Impossible Possible. Ada: Baker Books, 2015.

mother and father named him "Nebeyu," which means "prophet."

When Neb was in the orphanage at age ten, long-term missionaries Joey and Destiny arrived in Ethiopia to partner with Covenant Orphanage. They were doing ministry and shepherding the street kids. Every week they visited Covenant Orphanage and taught the children. They held Bible studies, worship, prayer meetings, field trips, and spent quality time there. The children grew to love Joey and Destiny and looked forward to the days they visited. After about a year with the kids, prompted by God, they adopted two older girls, Ayni and Anna. They said yes to God. They also fasted and prayed for a family for Neb. Joey and Destiny were not willing to adopt the two older girls, leaving the oldest boy still without a family.

Destiny and Joey created a photobook of the kids. Joey wrote Neb's bio and posted a picture of him. He professed openly that Neb had the gift of prophecy. They prayed and fasted for him. When they visited the United States in 2009, we loaned them our Chevy Avalanche to travel the summer and speak. They arrived at our house for dinner and shared the most beautiful stories. The days weren't long enough to hear all the tales they shared about how God was bringing children into forever families. Rick and I hadn't yet discussed adoption, but Rick met Joey and Destiny in Ethiopia, and his life was forever changed. When Joey and Destiny went to leave that night, Destiny and I embraced. As we held each other tight for several minutes, something felt different.

I learned years later about something Destiny dreamed before traveling to the USA. While they were still in Ethiopia, continuing in prayer for a family for Neb, Destiny dreamed about a trip she would make to the United States of America, and while on this trip, she hugged Neb's adoptive mom. In her vision she knew the hug felt different from any hug she ever experienced. When she awoke from her dream, she thanked God for the promise of Neb's family. That vision was God's way of confirming to her that God had a family for Neb. Destiny didn't realize the hug would be the defining moment of that promise, until it was. She never told Rick or me, but when she got in the car to leave us, tears filled her eyes. She turned to Joey and said, "I just hugged Neb's mom."

She was right! They left the book so Rick and I could pray over the children. The picture and bio of Neb is exactly how we knew he would be our son. God spoke to me by allowing me to envision Neb in the family picture on the fireplace and spoke through Destiny in a dream.

When we are open to "hearing from God," He speaks to us in different ways. I used to think when people said, "I heard from God," they meant an audible voice. Let me reiterate this. I have yet to hear an audible voice from God. Maybe someday, I am hopeful, but I do hear from God multiple times a day through His word, people, nature, music, dreams, visions, and journaling. He speaks with a still, small voice that shows in picture form.

God talks to Neb through dreams, prophetic dreams that often bring strength and comfort to others. Joey prophesied over Neb, then a ten-year-old boy, and much of what he envisioned came to pass. He shared that when Neb came to America, he would go astray. He would walk away from God, but he would come back stronger and use his gifts to show God's love. I have seen this to be true in Neb's life. Neb has shared with me multiple dreams that have come to fruition.

My favorite dream is the one he had in Ethiopia in 2018, when he was visiting his orphanage for the first time since his adoption.

True love was realized in a dream Neb had while visiting Ethiopia. He wrote it down, but he didn't tell anyone until he returned home.

Neb stayed in a bedroom at the orphanage where Joey and Destiny's adopted daughters lived as children. A picture hanging on the wall of this room caught his attention. It was of Anna, previously called "Kelemua."

Anna was adopted, along with her sister, by our missionary friends, Joey and Destiny. We had seen them a couple of times since their adoption. They lived in Fresno at the time, and Anna attended cosmetology school. Anna and Neb were friends on social media, but they had not kept in touch much.

Neb shared this story. He said as he closed his eyes to sleep his last night in Ethiopia, right before he fell asleep, he was looking at Anna's picture. He says he had a vision and heard, "You are looking at a picture of your wife. Anna will be your wife."

When Neb woke the next morning, he believed God had given him another prophetic dream, and he held this one close to his heart. He didn't try to figure out the details. He didn't tell anyone yet. He didn't say anything to God other than, "Yes, Lord, Your will be done."

When Neb was in his rebellious state, he wandered away from following God. He ran off track in many areas of his life, walking in sin with alcohol, pornography, and ungodly music. During this time of rebellion, Neb kept telling me he was going to marry a blonde girl. It wasn't the color of hair that made him rebellious. It was how far from God he had wandered that brought me to my knees for a couple years. I felt like all I did was pray for my big boys to surrender their lives to God. They both were so reckless for a time; I began to wonder what we did wrong. Their rebellious hearts took Rick and me both by surprise.

Before their junior year in high school, we thought as parents we were doing so well, we could write a book on parenting. Then came their junior years. That's when we realized we still had a lot to learn.

No book could help our boys turn their lives back to Jesus, but prayer certainly did. When Neb returned from Africa, after his visit in 2018, he called Joey. He asked permission to visit and stay with their family over spring break. He wanted to share about his trip back.

I noticed the change right away. Neb experienced so much healing during that trip. It was truly miraculous to see his heart on fire for God once again. He prayed and worshipped just as he had when we first brought him home. He visited the Ethiopian church and made new connections. Before we knew it, he was on his way to Fresno. After that trip, he was on FaceTime with Anna. Every. Single. Day. Not a day went by they didn't talk.

Neb still hadn't shared his dream with us, so we just assumed the two of them were growing together and processing their childhood with one another. Of course, they were doing that, and they were the best for one another. They could absolutely relate. When Neb told us Anna was coming to Sacramento to take the national cosmetology exam, we offered to host her. We planned a very special dinner at our favorite Ethiopian Restaurant.

Two days before Anna arrived, I received a text from Destiny.

It read, "This could really happen."

Really happen? What?

I couldn't wait. I called her. That's when she told me about Neb's dream.

I learned Neb shared his vision with Anna, and apparently, she laughed at him. However, Destiny believed something amazing was happening between them because both Anna and Neb were healing more each day. She noticed a difference in Anna, and I perceived a change in Neb. Love was in the air, or was it? *Could this really be happening?*

If Neb had this dream, then I absolutely believed it would happen. Nebeyu means prophet. Several dreams he had shared with me in the past had already come true. Was something wonderful about to happen?

Whether it is a dream, a vision, or the audible voice of God, prophesy edifies and encourages our faith.

Sacrificial Giving

How many times have you been told it is better to give

than to receive? I don't know if that phrase sinks in as a child, or maybe it doesn't even sink in as adult. However, when it finally becomes your truth, it is usually after you have given something life-changing. We want to live like Jesus. We want to lay our lives down and give our all, but that is impossible without understanding the gospel. We cannot give it all without the help of the Holy Spirit. We do not have the help of the Holy Spirit until we have received the gift of Jesus Christ. If you have never met the perfect Giver, I want to introduce you to Him now. Jesus Christ gave His all for you and for me. He did. He promises that He has made a way for you to be forgiven, made righteous, reconciled to a perfect Father in heaven, and made holy so you can have a relationship with God.

While we were living a sinful life, remember Jesus Christ died for us. He lived the perfect life with no sin, so He could be the living sacrifice we needed. He gave it all. There is not a set of rules you can follow to make you right before God. The only thing that makes you right is to accept what Jesus did on the cross for you and me. His bloodshed washes away all our sins—past, present, and future. His grace saves us for eternity, and all who believe will be in eternity together. I may not meet you on this side of heaven—although I would love it if we did—I will be with you for eternity. My biggest prayer and hope for every person who reads this book is that they will know and receive Jesus Christ. That they would let Him overwhelm them with His forgiveness, love, and generosity.

Angelica, my sister-in-law, lives life with this kind of generosity. I have been overwhelmed by her love so many times I could write an entire book on just that. She once gave me a gift that changed my life forever. The gift she gave me is something that I knew was priceless to her.

Angelica wore a gold angel ring on very special occasions. This ring caught my eye every time I saw her wear it, and eventually, I asked her where she got it. I stared at it in "awe" and admired its beauty. When she told me her dad bought it for her high school graduation, my eyes overflowed with tears. She knew me intimately, and she didn't even need to ask why I was crying.

She knew.

My biological dad had just been sentenced to life in prison, and I was not okay. To say this was a difficult time in my life is an understatement. I questioned God because I had prayed and believed in the best outcome for my dad. But the opposite happened. I knew my dad was not guilty of all he was accused, so to see justice not served devastated me. I still can't wrap my mind around the situation, but I have slowly learned to trust God anyway. I've learned to place my hope in eternity, where I am confident I will spend forever with my dad.

We were wrapping up our last night of Bible study when Angelica handed me a gift. We had studied generosity, and each of us was practicing living this selfless act of giving, even when it was costly to us. We each took the challenge and pulled a name from a cup. We were to prayerfully consider a gift to give the following week. We were challenged to give a gift we already had. We were not to spend any money, but to pray and give something that would be a blessing, even though it didn't cost money.

We knew He might put it on our hearts to gift something valuable, meaningful, or precious to us, but we said yes to the challenge of obeying whatever He spoke. We knew it would be a sacrificial gift.

I'll never forget what I felt compelled to give. I had a large Coach tote from my previous job. It was still in the beautiful brown box it came in, with tags still attached. I knew the value of the tote was nearly $500, more than I had ever spent on any purse or bag. I still had little kids, and I didn't want to use the tote until they were older, fearful I would ruin it with dripping baby bottles and revolving Goldfish snacks. I set that brown and gold box on the top of my closet and dreamed of the day I would pull it out. I prayed about what to gift to Mary Jane. When I looked up, it became clear. The Coach tote would no longer be mine. It was a sacrificial gift for me because I knew the value, and I had "earned" that bag as the top sales associate of our company that year. I gave the tote away anyway, and I never missed it. It felt good to gift someone else something valuable to me.

I did not know at the time Angelica had drawn my name. I was surprised she didn't tell me because we don't usually keep secrets from one another. She was the last one to present her gift to the group. She stood up and tears fell freely from her eyes. She's not a crier, so I knew this was hard for her. She began to share, and she said the second we talked about this challenge, she felt God tell her she would be giving me the gold angel ring. She knew it before she even pulled my name from the hat. When she opened the slip of paper and read "Wendi," it was a done deal. Angelica gifted me one of the most meaningful gifts ever given to her. There wasn't a dry eye left in the room. Sacrificial giving is never easy. In fact, often when God asks us to give, it doesn't feel "better" than receiving. That ring is still one of the most important gifts I've ever been given. I felt more love in her sacrifice than anyone else could have shown me in some of the darkest days of my life. Angelica loves me so much, that even though she is very private, she gave me permission to share the letter she wrote to me with all of you:

January 13, 2010

Dear Wendi,

While the cup was being passed around with the names to be drawn for this challenge, I must confess that I was hoping for someone I knew well. I figured it would be "easier" to come up with something to give to her. The second I drew your name, it hit me…this is not going to be easy; God is going to have to show me! I simply said in my head, "God, what of mine would you have me give her?" And at that moment, sitting there in your living room, I knew it was all a part of a bigger picture. I felt a lump in my throat…of course he would ask me to give you something that means sooo much to me! This is to be a reflection of how much YOU mean to me, and even further, how much we each equally mean to God.

When I got home, I was thanking God for what he was showing me through this particular act of giving, and allowing me the opportunity to take part in it. During my quiet time that day is when I came across this poem. I found myself crying at my computer as I read it. I often times forget to tell the people who are closest to me how I truly feel, and this poem COULD NOT express my feelings any better.

Wendi, thank you for who you are to me ... you are an angel in my life! Let this be a reminder every time you wear it just how much you mean to me, all of us in this room, but most importantly, God! Be blessed!! I love you!!!

Angelica- (She also included the lyrics of "My Sister, My Friend" by Leann Stiegman in the letter. Go check it out!")

Who wouldn't feel loved receiving such a gift? I wear the beautiful gold angel ring to every speaking engagement and writing event. Maybe you have seen it on me? This gift is a gift that keeps on giving. It is a reminder that God has surrounded me with His angels and that He, indeed, meets my every need. I am loved by many, but most importantly by God. May you believe the same is true for you.

You Can Do It

We sacrificed so much building our home in Drytown, CA, and walked in faith as we understood this place was our next mission field. We sold our large, beautiful home in Elk Grove, walked away from a backyard surrounded by pine trees, a built-in pool, covered patio, and outdoor kitchen—a backyard we shared with hundreds of people over the years, celebrating holidays, hosting worship nights, and gathering friends and family. A dream to own had been offered to us by my brother, and we just couldn't pass up the opportunity to expand into more space.

Owning forty acres on private, quiet, country hilltops where we could gather our quickly growing family was what he had hoped for all our lives. Deer, turkeys, eagles, and wild peacocks pass by nightly. Our wrap-around porch is a place to sip a cold beverage on a hot day or coffee and tea on a cold morning. The sunsets, sunrises, and views are breathtaking. I imagined respite and peace, calmness, and reward. Then God reminded me, "This house is not your house."

Everything on this earth is temporary and borrowed. We can work hard and earn the things we want, desire, and need, but those things can be taken in the blink of an eye. We can sacrifice, as we did for over eight months living in a hundred-year-old cabin with no air conditioning, no heat, no insulation, and a rat infestation. We went days without power and water at times, but we looked ahead to the reward of our new home, and we pushed through. It gave us a glimpse of what it is like to look forward to our forever home in heaven.

I didn't know if we could make it after being in the "love shack" for three months. We had occupied the cabin after nine years of it being abandoned, and we cleaned it as best we could. We hired electricians, contractors, and pest control professionals. We knew it would be a tough six months, but we decided as a family we could do just about anything for half a year. We realized after month three that living in the shack was going to be longer than expected. We had not even broken ground on our new home.

Cooper descended from his space in the loft, also known as his "bedroom," which could only be accessed using a ladder made by some cowboy in the 1800s. He was holding a pair of brand-new wrangler jeans with a large hole. "Mom, oh my gosh, the rats chewed through my jeans!"

I was so angry I could have spit nails. Instead, I walked into my room, got on my knees, and prayed, "God, please, if it is your will for us to live here, I have one prayer that MUST be answered. Please get rid of the rats."

In my own attempt to negotiate with God, I made a deal, "Lord, if you can get rid of the rats, we will stay. If not, I need to figure out something else." I was not trying to be a brat. I was more concerned with the health and safety of my children.

Colby, our oldest son, is always up for hard work. I called him and offered him a side job to help me clean out the attic. We had requested a quote from a professional rat removal company, and it was $4,000. The owner of our little "love shack" couldn't invest in that, and we didn't expect her to. She was doing us a favor by allowing us to live there.

Colby and I took the risk. We masked up with layers of facial coverings and climbed up the ladder to collect eighteen large black garbage bags full of old insulation. Breathing was difficult. We sweat bullets and itched all over. We took some breaks and came down for cleaner air. It was a dirty and daunting job, but we did our part. We destroyed multiple rat nests and set new traps. We went around the cabin, and on the roof, we plugged every hole we could find.

It was about two weeks later when we checked the traps, and sure enough, we caught our culprits. Between my plea to God, our hard work, and a whole lot of prayer, those rats were eradicated. We stayed in that shack until our house was built. We realized how much we took for granted as we all huddled and cuddled around the wood stove in the winter and gathered in the only room in the summer with a door and a portable air conditioner. We couldn't have multiple electrical items on at the same time or we would blow a circuit. We couldn't take long showers or water the lawn or our well would go dry. We were persevering through some very hard living conditions to have our dream home.

It Is Not Mine

You can only imagine my "expectations" as I dreamed about moving into our brand-new home. I was looking forward to quiet, peaceful, new, and clean. I was imagining our family on our "new" sectional watching a movie. I envisioned dinners on the back patio with worship music playing. I was imagining my kids finally having their very own rooms. Pictured decorating, organizing, and making my home "perfect."

Rick and I lay in bed a few months before leaving the "love shack," and he said, "I have it on my heart to consider offering my brother and his family the opportunity to move into our new house with us for a year while they save money to build their home."

What?!?

I'm so embarrassed to write this, but I cried. Not because of the "who" we were going to be helping, but simply because all the "dreams" I had been imagining were just ripped from my heart.

Fear come over me immediately, "Our house will get

destroyed." I went from imagining peace to having it replaced with thoughts of chaos. I went from thinking our eighteen months of sacrifice is almost over to realizing we could be sacrificing our comforts for another year. I went from imagining my kids in their own rooms, to bunk beds and multiple people in all the rooms. I panicked.

"Rick, I can't even think of that right now. You truly did just burst my bubble."

He began to explain how much help, how much support, how many people have helped us to get to where we are.

"We could be that help to Willy's family."

He was not wrong, but it took me a few days to process. We ended the conversation that night when I said, "You know, if God calls us to this, I wouldn't say no. I just need Him to work on my heart." I knew right after that comment, I would be getting a heart transplant. I did, and rather quickly.

I repented for holding my home in a tight grip. I was very quickly reminded this new house was not "mine." My favorite scripture is James 1:17, *"Every good and perfect gift comes from above."* Our new house was indeed a gift from God, and it is like any other gift, to be held with an open hand, and used for the glory and honor of God. Like they say in Uganda, "You are welcome." This means, "Come on in and stay!" We mean it, and we live it. "Mi casa es su casa."

14

OUR RETURN TO ETHIOPIA

"For I know the plans I have for you," declares the Lord, "plans to give you hope and a future. Then you will call on me and come and pray to me, and I will listen to you" (Jeremiah 29:11-12).

On Mission Together

I asked Neb year after year to join me on a mission trip back to Ethiopia. Year after year, he was not ready. He declined the invitation for eight long years. I waited. I trusted God. I prayed and surrendered to God's timing. Of course, I knew there were some strongholds in Neb's life that were deeply rooted in unbelief. I understood that some of his insecurities truly came from the lies he believed.

I prayed and believed if Neb returned to his birthplace, visited his family, walked through the dirt roads of his village, and encountered his culture for himself, his chains would be broken and truth revealed.

This would be no picnic. I knew it would be hard work, emotionally and spiritually. Our trip to Ethiopia in 2018 was all of that and more. We took photos and videos, made precious memories, and gained stories galore to share. We love visiting and speaking at colleges, high schools, churches, workshops, conferences, small groups, and ministries about adoption, family, biracial challenges, marriage, and missions. We love sharing and invite others into our "mess" to share our "message."[1]

It Takes a Village

I thought I might vomit from the overwhelming stench coming from all those bodies crammed into such a small space. Anyone who struggles with claustrophobia might have dropped dead from the sheer stress of the thirty people practically sitting on top of one another in a fifteen-passenger van, and more stood in line to board. If the space didn't get them, the smell might.

I chose to sit in the last row at the back, joined by three farmers who decided to share my bench seat, already occupied by me and four others. Farmers are my jam. Raised on a dairy farm, my childhood felt rich with the hard work balanced with outdoor fun. Riding horses, waking at the crack of dawn, milking cows, mucking stalls, and other farming and ranching activities created a strong work ethic within me.

Farmers in Ethiopia work long hard days, too. From

---

1 To book a teaching or speaking engagement for one or both of us, please visit www.xhopemissions.org/guestspeaker.

sunup until sundown, they toil hard to survive, and many make as little as $1 a day. My aversion wasn't to the farmers, but the smell of manure covering their clothing, added to the odor of the bodies in the jam-packed van, overwhelmed my system. I didn't expect this type of up close and personal travel when Neb and I agreed to join his older sister, Tigist, for dinner in her home. In fact, because none of us spoke Amharic, Neb's sister came to escort us. She sat up front and gave the driver directions on where to drop us. From my seat in the back, even if I had known the language, I could not understand anything the people said. Most assumed Neb knew the language, but once they realized he didn't, they became offended, even angry at Neb. This response shocked me and was one of the hardest parts of our return trip. The elders didn't want Neb to forget his language, but when adjusting to life with us, Neb chose to speak only English. We encouraged him to listen to Amharic music, write in Amharic, and read his Bible in Amharic, but that lasted about six months. When he knew enough English to tell us openly why he wanted to read an English Bible and listen to English worship music, we conceded. We trusted Neb knew what he needed, and we allowed him that freedom. We chose not to force anything. He is now learning fluent Amharic again and listening to that music. The conflict between adapting to life in America and keeping his culture was tricky.

The smell of the van was also tricky, the stench continued to nauseate me. I keep essential oils to rub on my wrists when getting car sick. I might as well have rubbed the entire bottle all over my body. Nothing worked. That van was one tough ride to the village, but so worth it once we arrived. Tigist married a Muslim man, so we were so excited to be welcomed into their home and to spend time with Neb's two-year-old nephew. From the food choice, it was obvious the meal they planned for us was a genuine sacrifice for them. My nieces and Pastor Molech from the USA joined Neb and me on this trip.

Tigist and her husband welcomed us into their small clay and brick home, decorated with beautiful linens. Gorgeous, beaded pillows for sitting surrounded a colorful mat where dinner would be placed. Spices unfamiliar to me reached my nose and smelled delicious, a welcomed contrast from the van ride over.

Before dinner, we received the traditional washing of hands in ceremonial fashion. Tigist walked around with a small basin and warm water. She poured the water slowly over our hands, and we rubbed them together. The extra water dripped into the basin under us. Once all our hands were cleaned, they invited Neb to pray over the meal. Even though we were sitting in the home of Muslims, they honored us by allowing Neb to pray in Jesus' name.

They included us in everything. We arrived with gifts from America, but they went to the market and purchased spices we did not have, lentils, and a large tray to serve Ethiopian food—all thoughtful gifts unique to Ethiopia. The generosity of the culture in Africa always blows me away. It's humbling to be on the receiving end when it is obvious they live on so little.

We once visited a church in Uganda and shared about

our children's home. This church gathered outside Entebbe. I learned of so much good coming from this church, but never dreamed we would be a recipient of such kindness. After I shared about our children's home in Jinja, Uganda, their pastor stood and took up an offering for us. So humbling. My heart stirred when he said to his congregation, "We need to be taking care of our own children. These people are here equipping us. Now let us show them we are willing to care for the orphans. I want to send Redeemer House Children's Staff home with anything we can gather. This is an offering, and 100 percent of what is given today will be sent with xHope to deliver to the children."

As I watched in complete awe, people began to remove their shoes and take them to the altar. Ball-point pens, coins, clothing, and even a pig were later brought for us. Throughout the night, people walked to the pastor's house carrying more things for the children. We were there to give, but God showed us what it is like to receive. It is more difficult to be on the receiving end.

Receiving from Neb's sisters was very hard for me because I knew how little they had. I also knew gifting to Neb was one way they could show their love. They wanted us to leave Ethiopia knowing they love us. They wanted us to always remember them and to make memories with us. Mission accomplished.

After our dinner together, they came with us back to Covenant Orphanage to help us translate. They were happy to walk us around the village and the market reintroducing us to the friends of Neb's mom. Seeing those women greet Neb felt like what I imagine heaven to be when we are reunited with Jesus. The perfect love, laughter, tears, and rejoicing was as if these ladies were hugging Jesus himself. Neb was so loved in this village. His homecoming felt like a true miracle to them. They kneeled and bowed, giving God all the thanks and glory for keeping him safe and bringing him back to them. I stepped aside to watch. I left my camera going, and I shed many tears. The moment was so surreal for me, Neb, and every friend there.

One of the ladies who cared for Neb when he was little invited us into her home. As we walked through the village on our way there, we collected some street kids. These little guys were barefoot and wild, running the streets just like Neb did as a child. We are not sure where their parents were, but it didn't matter. They grabbed onto our hands, and they, too, were welcoming Neb home. In Africa, there is a saying: "It takes a village to raise a child."

We have found this to be just as true in America as it is in Africa. These little boys knew exactly what kind of manners were expected while visiting a village home. They removed their shoes, sat quietly on the couch, and only spoke to say "thank you" in Amharic when given fresh bread and tea. We enjoyed being there. The memories flooded Neb's mind, and he thanked the woman for welcoming him back into her home. What an incredible gift it is to return and thank those who once cared for you. Not everyone gets to do that, but thankfully, Neb did.

We also visited Neb's old school.

As an outreach, we took school supplies, games, and

toys. We gathered the kids and taught them games, and they taught us as well. We sang songs, danced, and blew bubbles. Before we left the states, Neb collected soccer equipment, including new jerseys, to bring for one of the local teams. We hosted a soccer clinic and did some conditioning with the team. We even played a scrimmage game in the pouring rain, and we walked back from the soccer field more in love with this village, this country, and with our God who redeems and restores relationships. We saw firsthand God's love for Neb through the people in his village. He was loved, and well cared for, even though he was considered an orphan. May we all be willing to invite little barefoot children into our homes for bread, or milk, or cookies.

Whatever we provide, we need to show we care because we are all children of God.

15

GO AND MAKE DISCIPLES

"Therefore go and make disciples of all nations, baptizing them in the name of the Father and of the Son and of the Holy Spirit, and teaching them to obey everything I have commended you. And surely I am with you always, to the very end of the age" (Matthew 28:19-20).

When Going Is Harder Than Anticipated

We completed a twenty-eight-day fast leading up to the trip, and we were expecting miracles. I felt a stirring in my spirit. I just knew this mission would be a turning point. It was a significant trip to Uganda for so many reasons. Although we canceled the last two trips due to COVID, we believed the new travel regulations and mandatory COVID tests before departing America would be enough. Our negative COVID results should set us on our way back to our friends and families in Uganda, so I thought.

Kyle, Vice President of xHope, and I had three pastors join us on this trip. Scott, our largest donor, planned to meet us in Uganda on Tuesday May 18, 2021. It proved to be an eventful trip.

Pastor Shane's luggage didn't make it. This created much delay when we arrived at midnight, Saturday May 15. We completed the baggage claim forms for lost luggage. As we finished up and collected the remaining eight, 50-lb. bags of supplies, we headed out of the Uganda airport with such joy and anticipation. As we proceeded toward the exit, a police officer stopped us to check our passports and vaccine records. It was there we learned our negative COVID tests from America would not allow us to enter the country.

The week prior to our arrival, the Ugandan Department of Health changed the policy, and every person entering Uganda was required to visit their testing site and permitted to enter Uganda only if they received a negative COVID test there. Although we were agitated at this delay and detour, we tried to make the best of it. We were shuttled to Peniel Beach Hotel, with our luggage brought in a separate vehicle. Uncertainty crept in. We all silently prayed for peace in the unknown. Patrick, our first college graduate from our children's home, and now the treasurer of Redeemer House, followed the shuttle and waited for us. We were told to expect the testing to take one to three hours. It took every bit of three hours before Shontell, Cara, Shane, and Kyle's names were called. They received their NEGATIVE test results and were free to go.

When Bad Goes to Worse

I knew something had gone terribly wrong when my

name was not called. I took the first test, and so I expected my results to be among theirs. I walked back to the testing site from the canopy of tents where we waited, playing cards to pass time. I asked to speak to someone. Brenda, the customer care representative, calmly stated, "We need to take your test over."

She timidly explained my test had been contaminated. I began to feel more and more frustrated, especially since Patrick had been waiting almost five hours in the parking lot.

They administered the second COVID test and promised me results should only take about fifteen minutes. It didn't. Forty minutes later, Brenda and Brogin, a medical tech, escorted me away from my team and into an unknown building. They explained a doctor would be in shortly to have a "small talk." I knew right then my fear of testing positive had come true. I was not sick, and had no symptoms, but I knew a positive test was possible up to ninety days after having COVID.

As I waited on the doctor, I did all I knew to do. I prayed and pleaded with God to be nearby. The fear set in for the first time, and my thoughts ran wild.

What if I am stuck in Uganda? What if their tests are different than ours and I cannot pass one?

I had a doctor's note from Kaiser explaining that retesting after recovering from COVID is not recommended, as one can test positive for up to ninety days. I tested positive because five weeks prior I had COVID. Although I had healed from it already, it was still in my system. I felt real fear. How many days would it take for all traces of COVID to be gone? How long would I wait before I passed a test?

I heard familiar voices. Kyle and Shane came looking for me. They had been waiting for me for forty-five minutes. Seconds later, an ambulance pulled up, lights flashing. The driver descended from the cab and pulled on his full hazmat suit. Yep. It was for me. They told me to get in the ambulance. They explained that I would be taken to a government hospital for treatment. I felt overwhelmed and intimidated by the presence of police and armed guards all over the testing site. Their purpose was to be sure every person leaving the grounds had a negative test. Otherwise, they were taken into custody, by force, if necessary if they didn't cooperate. I explained once again, with more desperation, about the letter from my Kaiser doctor. They responded to my plea, "You must see a doctor here and show him that paperwork, and then he can sign and let you go."

At this point, I had heard so many inconsistencies, I had no idea what would happen next. As my knees continued knocking and my body was overcome with fear, the armed men slowly walked in toward me. They were pointing guns and nodding their heads to load into the ambulance. This was not a suggestion. This was a mandatory "Load up, now."

Thankfully, Pastor Shane took over and asked questions, more calmly than I. He rode with me in the ambulance, and we arrived at a government hospital. Patrick and the team followed close behind. The doctor came out, read the paper, and refused to sign off on anything. He and the ambulance driver frantically called people who held greater authority from the Department of Health. They kept trying to figure out what to do next with this positive COVID patient from America who was refusing treatment. After I persistently refused treatment, they had no other option but to drive me back to the hotel/testing site. Upon arrival back the medical assistant allowed me to rent a hotel room on-site to get rest. It was 5:00 a.m. Exhaustion set in, and I needed rest. However, my eyes remained wide open with concern, and my body trembled with fear. I laid down on the blood-stained sheets, peering across the room at a large cockroach running from corner to corner. Safe under a mosquito net I tried to close my eyes. Sleep refused me. Kyle volunteered to stay with me, while Patrick took our team to our partner ministry, CSI. I felt overwhelming gratitude for Kyle's company because the anxiety and fear I experienced grew more and more intense. I know scriptures to quote. I know God's promises. I know God is with me. Even so, in this very unknown situation, my options felt bleak.

We met with a medical technician named Brogin who was helpful. He seemed to understand the letter from America and tried his best to explain it to doctors. Unfortunately, he didn't possess the power or authority to fix anything. I wanted rest, but I was physically and mentally unable to relax enough to sleep. We stayed awake and prayed. All of us. We prayed with high hopes I would test again in the morning, get negative results, and get on with our mission.

We were wrong.

The Commander of the Department of Health arrived on site and called us out around 10:00 a.m. for a meeting. The morning COVID test I took was NOT NEGATIVE. This meant I could not leave the site unless driven in an ambulance to a nearby hospital for treatment. The Commander tried to explain why he must retain me, and he was also doing his best to understand the letter from America. However, that letter in Uganda validated nothing. It is a simple NEGATIVE or POSITIVE test that determines if we entered the country or not. Kyle and I realized the desperation of the situation. We then asked the Commander if I could willingly return home to America. He agreed, and we jumped through all the hoops to get away from the testing site. There is no way out of this site without a negative test, I was stopped once again at the gate trying to exit. Armed guards and police officers questioned us. The American presumably tested positive for COVID, and this caused so much suspicion. Some believed I was trying to flee, and the fear this caused was paralyzing. They were terrified of my positive COVID and fearful of my escape, and I was terrified for my life. I felt the heat rising, building from the toes up, when once again the commissioner and the doctor were called to the security gate, trying to work their political angle to get me back to the airport.

Twenty minutes passed. It felt like an eternity under their interrogations. Afterwards, it seemed we'd made a breakthrough. The police escorted me to the airport. I felt my fear growing, again. I knew it was a long shot for the airlines to accept my COVID test from America, especially now that it was six days old. The tests are only valid for 120 hours. I worked hard to negotiate, explain my letter from America, and show my expired COVID test, only to wait from 4:00 p.m. to 8:00 p.m. and be rejected. Now, I was at the Ugandan airport alone. It was dark once again. I needed to decide, based on faith, where to go from here. God had to protect me because I had no way to protect myself. Our team in Kampala at the CSI, texted me via messenger the entire time. I kept in touch while in the airport because of Wi-Fi. Unfortunately, I had to leave the airport with the Health Department and return to the testing site. I had no other option. As soon as we left the airport, I lost access and any ability to reach anyone on my team.

I called the Commander again, panicking. He promised he would get me on the flight, but even his authority fell short of getting me on any airline without a NEGATIVE test. His Department of Health employees kindly returned to pick me up. I endured interrogation by airport security three times during my wait. They asked questions and took copies of my passport. I sensed the chaos ensuing. I knew this was not going to end in my favor.

I continued to pray for safety until the Commander's employees arrived to take me back. They escorted me out of the airport and saw the guys I recognized from the testing site. As we attempted to back out of the parking spot, another police officer and airport security blocked our way and demanded we exit the car. They pounded on the window and told us to step out. They had guns drawn, and they asked more questions and required the

Commander's employees to show their official name badges. Then they asked for my passport, photographed it, and demanded I be taken immediately back to the testing site. They were very confused as to why I had tried to return back to America only twenty-four hours after arriving to Uganda?

Believe it or not, I was oddly relieved to finally return to the high-scrutiny testing site. Barbed wire fence in corkscrew shapes layered the top of the gated facility. Even though I was afraid and anxious, it was familiar. The hotel room I occupied the night before appeared now in arm's reach. I knew I could lock myself in and pray for peace, safety, and a way home to my family. I was going to be all alone in a hotel room, surrounded by the military, with time to communicate via Messenger once again with family.

We had another meeting under an avocado tree the following morning, surrounded by armed guards. Commander apologized for not yet getting me home.

"The airlines failed me," he said.

Although he tried his best to help me, the rules with TSA were black and white, no loopholes. One must have a negative test to board a plane flying out of Uganda. He, the Commander's employee, and Dr. Kenneth required that I stay self-quarantined on-site in the hotel and test again the following Tuesday. I faced seventy-two hours more of waiting. They assured me I would be safe there because they, too, were on-site. I paid $50 per night for a room and tried my best to find sleep.

Quarantine

The first night alone was so intense and intimidating. I couldn't unwind and sleep. The jet lag didn't help. I wanted and needed rest, but the war within grew harsh. The spirit of fear raged against me. Only the word of God and the power of the Holy Spirit calmed me. All the things I found comfort in at home such as food, television, and sleep, no longer served as a source of relief. My only comfort at that time was Jesus. I read the Word, memorized scripture, journaled, listened to worship music, and constantly prayed against fear. I laid my head on the pillow only to jump up startled by the men's voices out my window. I hid under my mosquito net, sat cross-legged, and rocked back and forth to the song, "Always," by Shane & Shane.[1]

It seemed an impossible situation, clearly where God placed me so He could make the impossible possible.

My Kaiser paperwork indicated repetitive COVID testing was not recommended because the tests could return positive results up to ninety days after someone recovered from the virus. My thoughts ran wild.

If this is true, I am hopeless. How will I get home? When will I be free to return to America to my family? Would the US Embassy need to intervene to get me home?

I needed a miracle. I needed a negative COVID test, yesterday!

During my time alone I wrestled with God, the Holy Spirit reminded me of my real needs. I needed to rest

---

1   Shane & Shane. "Always." 5, The Worship Initiative, Vol. 4. 2014.

under the shelter of the highest God and know He was with me. I needed to believe He had gone before me, and He would never leave me or forsake me. Even though I was being tested, God still was my refuge, and He was enough.

Still Alone

On the second day, I felt hope. Kyle worked out the details with Commander for Mebra, our Redeemer House social worker and a dear Ugandan friend to me, to come and stay with me until my release from quarantine. Kyle and the team felt more confident in my safety, so they proceeded on mission more than six hours away.

Then hope fell. Commander could not allow Mebra to stay there. He explained that exposing an otherwise unexposed Ugandan to me in quarantine was against policy. Oh, the disappointment! My heart dropped at the thought of spending one more night alone in a foreign land.

I prayed the team out on mission would experience all God planned for them. When Kyle made the difficult decision to proceed on mission, he felt confident there was nothing more he could do to help me. It became clear to us all only God could change this situation. We needed God to miraculously heal my body from any trace of COVID. We needed a negative test. I didn't want the entire trip to be ruined because I was locked in a hotel room, made military testing site, with no sure time of being set free. I also prayed for my faith to grow stronger, for me to trust God more, and for me to surrender to His will, without fear.

I keep asking myself, "Is He enough?"

He Is Enough

On day three, fear began to lose its grip. I began to see God's favor even during the lockdown. My staff in Uganda called to tell me, "We will not take anything, and we are praying all night long. We are trusting God to make a positive test into a negative test tomorrow." When they said, "We will not take anything," that meant they were all fasting on my behalf. Prayer teams everywhere prayed for us, including my amazing Bible study ladies who I video chatted with earlier that day. Simon and Mebra dropped off vitamin C and Zinc, a Uganda cell phone to contact everyone, and some bottled water. The hotel delivered breakfast and gave me the password to the Wi-Fi. Finally, I could see my husband, daughter, mom, and stepdad by video chat.

My husband, always so strong, spoke with such courage to me. He trusted God totally, without expressing an ounce of fear. He encouraged me to rest, read, and write— all the things I always wished I had more time for when at home. My mom spoke truth and encouragement over me, and she was not nearly as terrified as I feared she would be. I received so many uplifting text messages, scriptures, and worship songs from friends and family. God reminded me, while He sent me to minister to others, I needed to learn to be ministered to as well. God helped me see the favor Commander showed me, and God gave me a heart to trust Him.

That night, I prayed the morning would present an

opportunity for me to share my faith with the Commander. Perhaps he needed to hear the gospel? Months before the trip, I asked God in my prayer journal to bring me "providential relationships" in Uganda. He did just that. I let Commander, his staff, and Dr. Andrew know if they ever visited America, I would gladly show them the hospitality they had shown me. I invited each of them to my home.

In the Waiting

The evening before I took my final COVID test I sent Commander a text thanking him for his concern, and for taking such good care of me. I let him know I trusted him. He replied to my text, "You are welcome. Just relax. Everything will be okay. Thanks for the invite to America and your warm heart."

While I waited, God actively worked doing many things. He worked to prepare me for more, grew my faith and the faith of all who prayed. He worked to build new friendships and presented opportunities for me to share the Gospel. My final morning at the testing site, around 10:00 a.m., Tuesday, May 17, I was invited to a private meeting with Commander and Dr. Andrew. Commander asked me details about my current plane ticket, which I had not changed. I was scheduled to leave Uganda May 28 with my team. I wanted his wisdom on if he thought it risky for me to test that day, get a negative result, and stay knowing I would be required to test again May 27 to leave the country.

After a few moments of thoughtful contemplation, he said, "We will test you tonight and tomorrow you can leave here with a negative test. You can move about Uganda and complete the work you have come to do. On May 27, you come back to my facility here, and Dr. Andrew will administer the same test to be sure it is negative, and you will fly home with your team."

That was my miracle!

Commander explained to Dr. Andrew exactly what he expected, then the waiting began for the 8:00 p.m. COVID test. This good news came as such a miracle, and a way to redeem what the enemy tried to steal away. I am reminded that no weapon formed against us shall prosper, so staying in Uganda to finish our mission trip became my desire once again. I traveled all this way. To leave Uganda out of fear meant the enemy won that battle, and I might have missed the miracles waiting ahead. I, by no means, thought God wouldn't do all He planned to do using others. He didn't need me, but I needed Him, and He reminded me of that. I want to live a life so courageous that I don't miss a single miracle.

Worth the Wait

It was a long day waiting for the test. The doctor scheduled to be in my room at 8:00 p.m. was late. However, at 8:15 p.m., another assistant of Commander showed up to report there had been a delay. The doctor wouldn't be back on site until 11:00 p.m. He assured me the swab would be taken at 11:00 p.m., and results would not be delayed. In the meantime, our management team at Redeemer House continued to fast, pray, call, and send worship songs. Benard, the manager of our children's home, called to inform me that Henry (our finance manager), Simon (our education coordinator), and he would be there waiting for me to be released the following morning. I felt their excitement to see me and began to imagine the joy we would experience after this long wait. It had been eighteen months since I visited Uganda because of COVID, so the delay at the testing site was agonizing. At times I feared I wouldn't see my staff at all. I continued fighting the battle of faith over fear. I used scripture, prayer, and worship songs. I reminded myself that *God is never late. His timing is perfect. He will not delay. He is already victorious. The battle is won. I will grow stronger in my weakness. I will have renewed strength in the waiting. Help is on the way. I will not fear because He is my refuge and strength.*

I knew hundreds of people covered me in prayer twenty-four hours a day. I knew heaven was filled with the prayers of my brothers and sisters, and an army of angels surrounded me there. I knew God answered my prayers to see miracles and to meet providential relationships. *Maybe Commander will serve on our school board someday in Uganda. Maybe he will visit America. Maybe God will use our friendship to bring him to the Lord.*

I reminded Commander, on my last day, that the Bible says all authority is assigned by God. I told him God hand-selected him for this very influential and important job. I asked how he had been handling the stress and weight of COVID in his country. He said at times, in 2020, he felt as though he would go mad because his people were hungry, and the whole world operated out of fear. I reminded him God brought him through it all, and he was doing a very good job. I found such a blessing to encourage Commander, and I am so grateful I was there with him.

Commander checked in on me at midnight to learn the doctor had not yet been back to take my test. He confirmed the doctor left for the death of a parent of one of his staff members. I started to lose hope until someone knocked on my door at 12:30 a.m. It was Brogin. Oh, my goodness, that was a face I was so excited to see. He was the only staff who had comforted me my first night there. He arranged for the hotel room instead of leaving me at the hospital. He demonstrated such compassion and kindness. I saw Jesus in his eyes. I immediately wanted to shout, HALLELUJAH!

Free at Last

Finally, the test was NEGATIVE! Brogin and Anderson knocked at my door at 2:30 a.m. Brogin said, "Please close your eyes, we have a surprise for you." His joy overflowed, and I knew they were there to deliver good news. I closed my eyes, and they presented me with the negative test as if gifting me with an award. I felt their relief and joy mirror mine. We discussed fear. I repented and told them when we operate out of fear, we lose our faith. They said they noticed how hard it was for me the first two days, and then how different I seemed that day. I told them I could only credit God. The renewed strength I felt could only be contributed to the Holy Spirit. We celebrated together with smiles, praises, and joy. I invited them to visit us in Jinja, to see the children's home, and meet our staff. We also planned to have Brogin come to our hotel May 27 to take our final test for the departure flight May 28.

This situation of isolation in Uganda reminded me so much of Paul, not nearly as traumatic of course, but the waiting. When Paul was in prison for two years waiting on God, he didn't waste his time. Instead, Paul wrote four letters: Philippians, Ephesians, Colossians, and Philemon—all writings we read for instruction and encouragement two-thousand years later. Sometimes, in the waiting, God is developing us, developing others, and developing a plan. To be free physically meant I walked out of that COVID camp greeted by my amazing staff, and I was able to fulfill the plans God had already prepared. I proudly showed the guards my negative test and looked up to see my staff running toward me with wide open arms. They were laughing and crying at the same time. I was shaking in my shoes, I had hives on my chest, and I laughed out loud with relief. To be free spiritually meant I could look back clearly and recognize when fear had been bigger than faith, repent, and be developed in the waiting. Sometimes being in the waiting room is right where God wants us so He may accomplish His plan in us.

16

GROWING FAITH

"Love is patient, love is kind. It does not envy, it does not boast, it is not proud. It does not dishonor others, it is not self-seeking, it is not easily angered, it keeps no record of wrongs. Love does not delight in evil but rejoices with the truth. It always protects, always trusts, always hopes, always perseveres. Love never fails" (1 Corinthians 13:4-8).

He Answers Prayers

I hoped Neb's dream to marry Anna truly came from God. My heart wanted this more than I wanted anything for Neb thus far. We call Anna our Ethiopian angel. She overflows with unconditional love and compassion, and she possesses such a quiet and gentle spirit. She loves the Lord with all her heart, walks confidently in her convictions, and is so pure. She prays often and worships God with her whole heart. Her character surpasses all we ever hoped and dreamed for our son, but it is indeed what I always prayed for. God answers our prayers, and Anna is a testament to this truth.

However, before the proposal, before Anna could have answered with an enthusiastic yes, God worked within her. Anna sought God and waited for His answer.

Sometime after I learned of Neb's dream and of Anna's plans to visit us for the weekend, I asked her in a half-joking, but half-serious tone, "So are you going to marry Neb?"

They video-chatted for months. Neb felt confident God spoke to him clearly, so he boldly made that known to her. At the time, she giggled at him but when I asked, she shrugged.

"I am praying and waiting on God, but He hasn't spoken that to me yet. I have to hear that for myself."

When a twenty-year-old young lady answers with such confidence of God's will for her life, there is only one response that comes to mind.

"Amen."

A few months later Anna visited again. We cleared out the upstairs room so she could stay with us a few days at a time. Neb in turn made time to stay in Fresno with Anna's family when his schedule allowed. As time passed, they spent more and more time together. My own excitement grew at the prospect of gaining this Ethiopian angel as our daughter-in-law. I daydreamed about little Ethiopian grandbabies. I prayed. "Please God, let it be."

One morning after one of Anna's visits as she prepared to return to Fresno, I heard her singing worship music in the upstairs room. Blessed by her outpouring of love for God, and her praise, I too began to sing from my room. I heard her open the door and call to me. When I entered the room, the joy in her heart beamed from her eyes. God had answered her.

"Yes, I am going to marry Neb. I was in a time of prayer this morning and God gave me a vision of Neb as a husband and father. He showed me that everything I've prayed for in a godly husband is who Neb will be. I am going to marry Neb."

Tears filled my eyes, and my heart pounded with excitement, realizing my daydreaming would become a reality. My son had been given the most beautiful gift in the world. I believed that and still do. A wedding was in the near future.

The Dance

I had already learned the dance, the one of becoming a mother-in-law, when Colby married.

Madison walked into my closet with joy and enthusiasm as she slowly pushed the hangers over one at a time, "Oh my gosh, I love your style so much. So, so cute in here."

Colby had told us all about this joy-filled, fun-loving beautiful girl from his college. He showed us a picture on Instagram and said, "Mom if she will date me, I'm going to marry her."

Colby was our first to launch from home to college. I remember the day we drove him to Corban University in Oregon, an answered prayer to see the many years of soccer investment finally pay off. Colby was going to play soccer on a sports scholarship, at a Christian school. It couldn't get any better, or so we thought.

We toured the school. We met the coach. We set up his

dorm. And we went to a chapel Sunday morning for the parents. I remember clearly the passage preached and message spoken. It was an encouragement to parents as they were driving away, leaving their kids at college for the first time, comparing this to Mary as she left Jesus at the temple. It was always meant to be, we raise them up in the way they are to go, and then we let them go.

One Kleenex box down, all the tears that could fall, and a quiet ride back home to California. I asked Rick, "Will I ever stop crying?" I knew everything about leaving Colby at Corban was answered prayers, God's will, and purposeful, but it didn't make it any easier for this mama's heart.

One year into his college education Colby began to have conversations with us about school. He continued to plant the seeds that college was not for him. He was very stressed. The academics were too much. He was feeling led to join the military. We were so confused as parents. We were afraid of what could be next. We began praying on our knees for his decision and hoped he would persevere and finish college. But we also wanted to support Colby.

It was year two of college and Colby asked to bring his girlfriend home to meet us. It was the beautiful girl on Instagram he had shown us pictures of six months prior. We were thrilled to have Colby coming home for spring break, and even more thrilled to meet Madison.

He boasted about her inner and outward beauty, and even with all his boasting, Madison was even more beautiful in person. Her smile lit up the room. Her laughter was contagious. She brought the fun—a perfect match for Colby.

The two were married and I learned to be a mother-in-law.

It was not an easy transition. Watching your children become one with their spouse, leave and cleave, and move ahead in life without you being right by their side to catch them when they fall is difficult. It's like a dance adjusting to this big change. Sometimes it's beautiful and sometimes we are stepping on one another's toes.

Colby and Madi RSVP'd yes to Casey's eighteenth birthday dinner at our favorite hibachi restaurant. Our family arrived to be seated, and lo and behold, two empty chairs remained. We waited. We texted. We called.

"Sorry we were just with you guys yesterday. We wanted to just spend time alone and rest. We are not coming."

I about lost my marbles. Anger flooded me. *Who does that?* I thought.

Colby had never before missed a birthday celebration for a sibling.

Rick looked at me and gently just shook his head no. He was telling me, "Not right now." I knew I needed to stay calm. I needed not to say anything I would regret. We were there to celebrate Casey, and he indeed is worth celebrating.

We let a week go by and then Rick and I had the family over once again for Sunday dinner and swimming. When Madi and Colby arrived, we talked to them. We let them know we were very disappointed that they said, "Yes, we will be there," and then they did not show up.

They explained to us that Madi had moved away from her family and missed them so much. Our family gathers often, and they felt overwhelmed, like they had no time to just spend alone. They felt too busy, too smothered.

Never did we want them to feel pressure about gathering

with us. Our intentions were always to invite them and let them be free to decide yes or no to the invitation. Once we communicated that, they seemed to receive it.

Stepping on toes is a normal part of learning to dance. Once we practice, correct the steps that do not work, and flow with the rhythm of one another, the dance is beautiful. It's like the night of their wedding when Colby and I shared the mother-son dance. It has been twenty-two years of stepping on toes, but that night, it was perfect.

Now, all these years later, we plan family dinners monthly and Madi and Colby are the first to arrive! They bring the fun. There is always a dance party to be had when the two of them are together.

Soon we'll learn a familiar, but new dance with Neb and his bride, but this time we have some experience learning new rhythms. I looked forward to these new steps.

Entertaining Angels

We planned a party for Neb's twenty-first birthday. Knowing Anna and her family would join us, we prepared an Ethiopian feast. This year presented so much to celebrate. Anna agreed to cook an authentic Ethiopian dinner, which quickly became our favorite way to celebrate anything. Hands down, she is the best cook and the only one we know who can create the most amazing authentic Ethiopian dishes—all of them. To say both families rejoiced in this celebration is an understatement, as Anna was the only one unaware of Neb's special surprise planned for the evening.

Opening our home is an important part of our ministry.

For years, Rick and I have practiced hospitality in our home. In fact, Anna's family stayed with us before we ever really knew them. From that early connection to grow into this union felt extra special.

Neb and Rick worked hard on a lighted sign to help ask the all-important question. At the right time, a larger-than-life 5x7 piece of plywood, painted all black, drilled with tons of tiny holes strung and filled with tiny white lights would illuminate the question.

As we videoed and sang "Happy Birthday" to Neb, Colby and Casey carried the board to the backyard. As soon as the song ended, Neb stood from his chair, took Anna by the hand, and led her to the sign. He then lowered himself down on one knee. At that moment, on cue, the lights came on. She read the words. Neb asked for her hand.

"Will you marry me?"

Gasping, Anna threw her hands over her mouth and tears began to fall. Unable to form one simple word, vigorously nodded her answer.

Yes!

Anna wasn't the only one crying tears of joy. We were getting our second daughter-in-law. Overjoyed, there wasn't a dry eye in the gathering. Anna was the perfect gift to Neb, and Neb the perfect gift to her—a match made in heaven, truly!

Heaven is something we dream about. We dream about the street made of gold and the perfection of heaven. We thrive on knowing there will be no more sin and no more tears. We envision the days there with no sickness and no death. It all sounds so magnificent, and I believe it all to be true. Heaven is where I want to be for eternity, and for all who believe in Jesus and what He has done for us, I'll meet you there. Matthew 6:9-13 starts off by saying, *"Our Father in heaven, hallowed be your name. Your kingdom come, your will be done, on earth as it is in heaven."*

How do we know His will on Earth as it is in Heaven? I personally believe if we read His word, we learn His will. We don't always do His will, but we know His will. I'm just glad in my own life I have experienced many, many do-overs regarding God's will. I'm thankful He is patient and gracious. I know God's will for us on earth is to feed those who are hungry, to comfort those who are lonely, and to do so means we might entertain angels.

Second Chances

I was in the McDonald's drive-thru in Las Vegas years ago. As I spoke into the speaker placing my order, I saw a homeless man sitting near the speaker. Instead of greeting him, I rolled up my window and pretended as though he didn't exist. After receiving my food, I saw him looking at me in my rearview mirror. Conviction hit me hard. I felt embarrassed and mad at myself, so I started asking myself questions. *Why was that my first instinct? Why didn't I offer to buy him something to eat?*

I wrestled and realized the answer. Fear. I rolled up my window and decided to protect myself in case the homeless man was dangerous. It sounded like a logical excuse, but I had been asking God to teach me to live like him for several years, so rolling up my window was a personal conviction. I repented, and I spoke out loud to God, "Please forgive me for operating out of fear. Please give me another chance, and I will do that differently."

The next chance to provide food for a homeless man happened at that same McDonald's a few weeks later. This time I had three of my kids in tow, my sister-in-law and her kids, and my best friend and her kids. We walked into the restaurant, and the kids all took off to the PlayPlace.

Play dates at McDonald's felt like a trip to Disneyland with nine kids under the age of eight. The near all-day event wore us all out but got us out of the house.

Walking up to the cash register I noticed a man who appeared homeless reading the newspaper. He didn't have food in front of him and was seated alone. He wore over-sized pants held up by a rope for a belt. His pale blue shirt was dirty and torn, and his black tennis shoes were un-laced. When I saw him, I immediately knew this was my second chance. I walked to his table and pronounced matter-of-factly, "Sir, I would like to buy your lunch."

Without showing his face from behind the newspaper he replied, "I'll take a $1 chicken sandwich and a $1 ice cream cone."

"Sir, you can have anything on the menu you want."

"I'll take a $1 chicken sandwich and a $1 ice cream cone."

I walked away and placed our very large order. I ordered nine kid's meals, three adult meals, a $1 chicken sandwich, and a $1 ice cream cone.

I anticipated the moment I delivered his meal, and my heart filled with thankfulness. God so clearly answered my prayer and gave me this second chance. I picked up the tray with his sandwich and carried his ice cream cone in my free hand. I placed the tray in front of him and extended my hand to give him the dessert.

"Jesus loves you," I said.

Before he took the cone, he lowered the newspaper, and my gaze met the most piercing blue eyes of what I believe to this day to have been an angel. He replied, very matter-of-factly, "I know He does, and He wants you to know He loves you too."

I froze. My knees shook. My face turned pale. My heart pounded. I turned and raced into the playland area to tell Angelica and Erin what had happened.

They stepped out to see the man seconds after I told them the story, but he was gone. When we entertain angels, we will probably never know we are, but when we ask God for second chances, we can be confident He will make that abundantly clear.

Hebrews 13:2 says, *"Do not forget to show hospitality to strangers, for by so doing some people have shown hospitality to angels without knowing it."* I love that our life consists of entertaining angels every time we get together. Anna is just one of the many angels we get to entertain.

17

NEVER GIVING UP LOVE

"Let the redeemed of the Lord tell their story—those he redeemed from the hand of the foe" (Psalms 107:2).

Redemption

I always thought my past would disqualify me, but now I know my past, in fact, made it possible for me to prove our God is a redeeming father. Now, I know if I can be forgiven, redeemed, and used by God, so can you. I didn't deserve the honor of being called "mother" to my six beautiful children. I am not qualified to be the director of a children's home and school in Uganda. I was not raised in a home where marriage was a forever commitment, but I couldn't be more in love with my gracious husband of twenty-five years. If my past defined me, I would be a teeny-tiny, rejected, helpless, insecure little girl who feared being alone. I would seek approval by performing to the best of my ability, yet putting aside my own hopes, dreams, and desires. I would please anyone with authority over me by being the best and following rules (when they were watching, at least).

My 4.0 GPA in high school led my parents to believe I was doing just fine. Little did they know, their recent divorce set me on the course of destruction. The divorce was a trigger for me to rebel. My behavior at the time was sneaky, dishonest, and hidden from my mom and dad, who loved me deeply. My parents loved my brother and me and would have done anything we asked of them, I just didn't ask. I didn't want help. I didn't know how lost I was. I was a teenager who took advantage of the situation and made very bad decisions. These decisions were not at all a reflection of my parents' love for me. They very well could be the result of brokenness and loss. My old self didn't believe in the love described in 1 Corinthians 13:4. My decisions and actions proved to the world I was seeking love. The loneliness I experienced my freshman year in high school triggered destructive ways I used to cope. Drunkenness. Sex. Drugs. Parties. Popularity. All I had to do to deceive my mom and dad was to keep my grades up, be awesome by the world's standards, and not get caught being naughty. I had my family fooled. I told them I was good. I acted good. In fact, I thought I was good at the time.

When I look back, I would give myself an A+ on acting the part. I acted the role all right. I performed like I was just fine all alone. And I remember telling my mom she should stay at her boyfriend's house so I could be alone, even though the loneliness affected my every thought. Although alone, I still had something to prove. I received academic awards, I made the high school cheer team all four years, and I was voted the secretary of the regional FFA club. I was the state champion for the speech contest. I made All-American and participated in the Macy's Thanksgiving Day Parade. Plus, I excelled at my job as a student assistant for the State of California. And I did it all with a smile on my face. It was impossible for even my parents to realize the turmoil inside my heart. I covered the fear of rejection by performing and being the best at everything I put my mind to. I believed if I was excellent, I would be accepted, and perhaps everyone would approve of me.

Not to Blame

I would never blame my mom or dad for the hurt I experienced, as I am aware, they too didn't know the kind of love described in God's word, yet. Not only did the divorce cause loneliness and insecurities, but it also caused so much confusion. No longer did I have the consistent influence of a loving father and protective brother speaking into my life. Instead, I had boys who told me what I wanted to hear, provided me with drugs and alcohol, and took advantage of me only to wake up the next day wondering if I had done the unthinkable. Had I slept with them or not? As I stumbled my way through high school, I built layers of bricks around my heart—each one cemented with regret—and I believed I had disqualified myself from ever living a healthy and happy life. I believed love didn't exist and if it did, I didn't deserve it anyway. I believed the lies about myself. I was a drunk. I was wanton. I was unforgiveable. Oh, I had done the unimaginable, and love was not possible. I couldn't be forgiven for all I had done. I was a hot mess. I had failed. I was hopeless.

Despite what I thought about myself and my many failures, God continued to provide new and exciting roads to travel. He led me up the windy highway from Sacramento to Reno, Nevada and provided me with a fresh start at the University of Nevada, Reno on a full-ride cheer scholarship. I had new friends, new ambitions, a new home, a new chance to perform. However, not learning from my past, I brought those failures and habits with me. Before long, the partying began, the drinking consumed my attention, and the same mistakes from high school became patterns for college. I excelled in my college classes. I made the travel team for cheer and even won second place in college partner stunt nationals. I was succeeding according to the world, but I was still missing the freedom to love and be loved. I lacked joy and confidence, although I appeared to be the most joyful and confident cheerleader you ever did see.

Love at First Sight

My outward appearance was just enough to draw the attention of a 6'6" defensive lineman named Rick Cross. Rick was the older brother of my stunt partner, Will Cross. Rick and I met one day when I drove his brother home to grab clean practice clothes. We walked into the stench-filled apartment and found six defensive linemen napping between football practices. They were sprawled out in their underwear, bellies hanging out, lying on couches, hardly able to move from the daunting "three-a-day" football practices. The apartment was the home of many young bachelors. The dishes were piled so high in the sink you couldn't use the faucet. The empty beer bottles and cans covered each tabletop. If recycled, those beer cans were worth a small fortune. The dirty clothes covered the floors, and the odor of sweat filled the house. It was so gross. Dirty. Nasty. And very unattractive. I had zero desire to know these popular football players, and I assumed they hadn't noticed me either.

Rick Cross did notice me. I was unaware at the time, but Rick told his brother, "That is my wife." Willy laughed it off and repeatedly told Rick I was not interested. He was right. I made a promise to myself I would not date a football player. I was not keen on dating my very persistent friend Rick until he decided to throw me a surprise birthday party. I walked back into the bachelor pad on September 28, 1997, and was startled.

"Surprise!"

Rick, a popular football player who had been there two years before me, knew athletes from every collegiate sport at UNR. He invited the swim team, the ladies' and men's basketball teams, the baseball team, the dance team, the cheer squad, and the football team. I walked into my surprise party and only knew the names of those in cheer with me—maybe twenty of the two hundred fifty-plus people crowding the apartment. I was not only surprised, I was speechless!

The amount of people there celebrating me was astounding, but what was more shocking was to find out why Rick Cross was throwing me this raging party. He wanted to date me, but his brother continued to tell him I was not interested. I had no idea, but Rick was relentless. I decided the morning after my birthday party, that man deserved a breakfast date.

Date one led to another, and another, and many more dates, many more parties, and eventually brought us to a marriage. And it soon gave us an unexpected mascot for our cheer and football team—Colby Branson William Cross, our first son, who made his appearance in the middle of our college careers. He became the toy in the men's locker room, passed around from player to player, and the joy on the cheer mats. We couldn't get enough of this little person, and we loved him the best way we knew how. We continued our cheer and football careers and graduated in 2000. Colby was nearly two years old, and our marriage was already on the rocks. Instead of partying together as we had in the past, we began to take turns going out. While I watched Colby, Rick went out, and the following night, we switched roles. Rick kept Colby and I went to parties. This lifestyle led to the destruction of our marriage and family. Rick and I were so close to divorce— the one thing we had promised we wouldn't do—we were going to do it. We were going to do what both his parents and my parents did. We were giving up on love.

Love Wins

Rick didn't want to give up, and he pleaded with me, "Babe, let's try church."

I was raised Mormon until the age of eight. Rick was

raised Catholic. In our personal experience, neither of those helped us much, so we decided to try a non-denominational Christian church. Rick knew the pastor of University Family Fellowship because this pastor prayed over the football team before games. I agreed to visit this church not knowing what to expect. I had never been to a church with such incredible music, a full band, and overwhelming joy. I had never been greeted with such kindness at a church. I had never seen a Christian community gather, love one another, and serve with such generosity.

I looked around, noticing the joyful laughter, the encouraging words, and the friendships. The music started, and I began to read the lyrics on the screen. I started to sing along when a lump in my throat formed, tears began to well up in my eyes, and my heart truly skipped a beat. The songs continued, and the words chipped away at the cement that formed the brick wall around my heart. I was astounded by the lyrics. I was in awe of the love these songs spoke of, and I was suddenly made aware of God's love for me.

I learned our mistakes could be forgiven and thrown "as far as the east is from the west." I heard the gospel preached, the good news of the perfect life Jesus lived, His death on the cross for me, and his victory over death when he rose three days later. And I learned He did this for me and that there was NOTHING I had ever done that would separate me from His perfect love. I learned He was not expecting me to get all cleaned up and to "perform" before He would accept me. Instead, I learned I was accepted "as is." So I wept that day. My husband was shocked that the brick wall I had built over time could be broken down by God's perfect love—the perfect love of Jesus. I was all in. I raised my hand. I prayed the prayer. I joined every Bible study available. I even joined the choir knowing I am tone deaf. I wanted to learn every song, and that was the fastest way to do it.

Don't worry; I learned later they turned my microphone off, so no one actually had to hear me.

It was the first time in my life where I began to believe I was not disqualified but accepted exactly as is. I learned even if everyone I loved left me, God never would. I learned the kind of love I had always hoped for was the love I could only receive by my Heavenly Father through the sacrifice of His perfect Son. This never ending, the never-giving-up love, was what I was finally receiving, and because I was receiving it, I learned to also give it. Although my past sins and failures defined me for some time, they do not define me now. I am loved. I am forgiven. I am set free.

Receiving the love of God and His forgiveness has been the reason our marriage has survived, and why our family has multiplied. Blessed with four biological children and two adopted children, we know it is God's grace alone that brought us to where we are today. The love we receive from God is the love we try to share with our children. Although perfect love cannot flow from us to them, it can flow from Him to them, and we point them there often.

In fact, it took us seven years of pointing our oldest adopted son, Nebeyu, to Jesus while fighting in prayer for him to receive our love just as we had received God's love. It was the never-giving-up love of God we showed Neb that led him to the healing hands of Jesus. The journey of getting Neb to this place was not easy, but it was worth it. He had reasons to fear attachment, reasons to be angry, and reasons to suppress his emotions. He was orphaned at a young age and survived things I couldn't imagine living through. God is good. He saved me from so much, but most importantly, He saved me from myself.

Today is the day. If you have not yet received the love of God and His forgiveness, will you do it now? Will you trust Him to heal you, free you, and redeem you? It's not a magic potion, but surrendering your life to Jesus is a magic moment. It's as simple as confessing with your mouth that Jesus died for your sins so you can be forgiven, and believing in your heart that He is your Lord. If you would like to accept Jesus as your Lord and Savior, you can pray a simple prayer like this:

Dear Lord, thank You for Your son Jesus. Thank You for sending him to live a perfect life because You knew I could not. Thank You, Jesus, for dying on the cross for my sins. I receive Your forgiveness. I would like You to be the Lord of my life. I confess with my mouth and believe in my heart You are Lord. I will follow You all the days of my life. In Jesus' name, Amen.

If you said that prayer today, the heavens are rejoicing. There is a party going on in heaven right now. I have goosebumps thinking of the joy and I can't wait to meet you in heaven someday. Welcome to the family! You just made the best and most important decision of your life.

18

DREAMS COME TRUE

"But the plans of the Lord stand firm forever, the purposes of his heart through all generations." (Psalms 33:11).

The Wedding

She walked down the sandy beach in her white-lace gown on the shores of beautiful, blue Lake Tahoe. Neb waited patiently in his black tuxedo, perfectly dapper, wearing a confident smile across his face. He knew she was his gift from God, and he received that gift in faith, with determination, and with confidence. The rest of us gasped at her beauty as she smiled, her eyes locked with Neb's eyes. He too was her gift from God, and she received him with faith, unconditional love, and joy. Her outward beauty shown like that of an Ethiopian angel and her inward beauty equally angelic. The two fell in love after a prophetic dream. Their marriage, their lives, and their wedding all represented God's perfect plans.

Neb and Anna prayed about their wedding plans. Clearly, every detail reflected great thought and intent.

Neb and Anna wanted to become one in the most God-honoring way. They planned a large wedding. However, COVID soon reduced the number of guests allowed to attend, but in no way reduced their joy and commitment to one another.

An intimate gathering of immediate family came together to witness the vows. Anna and Neb spent some time in live worship inviting the Holy Spirit and singing praise to God for His goodness, His faithfulness, and His perfect plan. They then invited both sets of parents to pray over them. What a true testament of their desire to honor God and to always cover themselves in prayer. We waited in anticipation for the couple to exchange their vows.

The Vows

Promises are made. Promises are broken. Some promises are kept forever. All of us want to keep our word, and at times we do. We all know many married couples who cannot look back on their vows with integrity and say, "Yes, I've kept every promise." We are human beings with the best of intentions, but marriage can be incredibly difficult. Life throws storms our way, and sometimes we lose track of where we are. Finances, children, trauma, loss, and addiction can break a marriage when, prior to the hardship, everything appeared to be just fine. We sin. We mess up. We make mistakes. Our promises, though heartfelt and pure, are not bulletproof. There is only One who can follow through without ever breaking a promise, and that is our Lord and Savior Jesus Christ. He is the only perfect promise keeper. This is why we need Him. We must rely on His power, His presence, His forgiveness, and His will.

As they read their vows and made promises to one another, Neb and Anna knew only with Jesus Christ would it be possible to keep them. As we witnessed the exchange, we felt as though we all stood on holy ground.

Now, it is on my heart to invite you in. I want you to read these heartfelt vows and feel the love between Anna and Neb. It is beautiful. It is also important for you to know nothing is as perfect as the love God has for you. May you know, as you read these vows, that Jesus loves you more perfectly than even this beautiful fairytale-like love of this precious couple. I give thanks to both of them for allowing us to share in these beautiful promises and remind us of the love that comes from Jesus Christ to one another.

Anna to Neb

Neb. I couldn't imagine anyone else standing next to me on this day. I remember when I got a phone call from you on your way back from Ethiopia telling me that God had told you that I would be your wife. To which, I laughed, and then thought "This is for sure a joke." Little did I know that moment would be the beginning of our love story.

I am beyond thankful you are the person God chose for me. You are everything I have prayed for and more. I love your heart for God and for people. I love your curiosity to always want to learn and grow. I love your compassionate heart and ability to see others for who they really are.

It has been a joy and honor watching you grow into the person you are today. I am so excited and look forward to starting our life together. I can't promise you that I'll be the perfect wife, or that I will never disappoint you, or that we'll never fight, but I do promise to always fight for you and never against you.

I promise to always be by your side to encourage you, to pray for you, and of course, to cook for you. I promise to grow with you. I promise to share your dreams. I promise to build a home that is filled with love, laughter, compassion, and good food. Above all, I promise to love you with all my heart and to keep God at the center of our marriage and everything we do.

Neb to Anna

Anna. Besides this being a perfect plan ordained by God, equally as important, you are everything I hoped and dreamed of as my wife. In fact, you know that you literally are my "dream wife." Do you remember the day that I told you, "You are going to be my wife?" you laughed at me, but who is laughing now?

Of all the things God has spoken to me in dreams, you are by far the most precious and valuable. I love you for so many reasons, obviously your cooking, but it's far beyond that. Your calmness, patience, beauty inside and out, your love for God, and your desire to give and serve others. These are all the qualities I pray we can raise our children to know and do.

I promise to protect you, serve you, and lead you in a way that honors God. I promise to carry your burdens and make them light for you. I will lay down my life for you as Christ has done for the church. I promise to always be faithful, merciful, forgiving and understanding. I promise to love you as much as humanly possible. I promise to always be devoted to God and you.

I couldn't be more thankful to God for this day and for making you my forever wife. You truly are my forever. I love you now, and I promise to love you forever.

Rainbows

As the vows concluded and Rick said, "You may now kiss the bride," we all had tears of joy. Those tears quickly turned into tears of amazement when God gifted us all with a beautiful rainbow. Being in awe was our reality as a large bright rainbow suddenly appeared over Neb and Anna. Only a God as amazing as ours would end His fairytale story of unconditional love and redemption with a rainbow, symbolizing His promise to never flood the earth again. We received this symbol as a promise fulfilled to both Neb and Anna. We remember it often in times of uncertainty, and we stand firm in the hope of Jesus Christ. May His promises be your hope too.

Rainbows are known as a symbol of hope in many cultures. Ethiopia. Uganda. Mexico. America. All the places we have gone to make disciples, evangelize, do mission, and build relationships. Regardless of "where" God has sent us, one thing remains true; we want to empower others by providing hope, love, education, and forever families. It is not the hope of us we want to share, but the true hope of our salvation through Jesus Christ. Like the rainbow, it appears after a rainstorm and signifies a beautiful promise from God to each of us. May you always see the rainbow and be reminded forevermore of God's love, redemption, and promises.

ACKNOWLEDGEMENTS

Thank you to my husband Rick Cross who has spurred me on to "Go and make disciples of all nations." The one who sends me and holds down the fort, cares for the kids, and sacrifices so much to give me the opportunity to be on mission. You have taught me forgiveness and grace. You have encouraged me and made me courageous and bold for Jesus. Every "yes Lord" is because of your selflessness.

Thanks to my fun-loving boys: Neb, Colby, Casey, Cooper, and Jay. Being your mom has been the training ground for our mission work. Each of you has always been my first mission. It has been my greatest joy in life cheering you on at every sporting event and showing up for each milestone. Memories flood my grateful heart. My deepest desire is that we always have fun making meaningful memories that honor God.

Thanks to my beautiful girls; my one and only daughter, Cami, and my angelic daughter-in-laws Madison and Anna. Cami, I prayed for you and waited on the Lord, and then I gave up hope after three boys. Your daddy convinced me to have one more baby. He was confident we would have our baby girl. Since the day you were born, we have had endless cuddles, laughter, and love. There are none like you, "sister." Madison and Anna, I have also prayed for you since my boys were little. I asked God to bring them Jesus-loving wives, woman who would make them better men, who would cover them in prayer, who would extend grace and who would help them to be the best daddies. I couldn't have chosen a better match for Colby or Neb. Thank you for embracing this crazy crew and making every family gathering so much livelier. And most of all, thank you for giving us the most precious gift in life, our grandbabies.

Stay tuned, blessings abound, as our twenty-one-year-old son is getting married this summer (2024) to an equally impressive and God-loving young woman, McKenna. They met and fell in love on our last mission trip to Uganda. Cooper soon to follow with his lovely and devout girlfriend, Jocelyn. Our cup runneth over (Psalm 23:5). Yikes!!

Thank you to Mom and my stepdad Steve, aka "Grammy and Papa." The many ways you've shown up for Rick and me over the years has strengthened, encouraged, and empowered us to fight for our marriage, to never give up on choosing love. The weekends you've kept the kids, the weekly date nights we have been able to enjoy because you wanted to spend time with your grandkids every Wednesday night. Every mission trip to Uganda when you stepped in to do all the driving, cooking, cleaning, and housework. We can do the work God has called us to do because of you. Mom, you're my angel and my best friend. I want to be just like you when I grow up.

Thank you to my dad and brother. As a little girl you built me up, and you are still encouraging me daily. You've spoken into my life and helped me to know my identity. You protected me always and gave me almost everything I asked for. Billy, thank you for eating the nasty things off my plate so I didn't have to, and for taking me everywhere you went. You were my first protector and best friend. Raising my family next to yours is a dream come true!

Thank you to my best friends in all the world. Angelica Cross and Erin Harrison, we have grown in our faith together and learned to follow Jesus together. We have celebrated the best of times with laughter, love and joy, and we have grieved the hardest of times with prayer, tears, and hugs. The one thing that has always remained true is that we want to see God fulfill the good work he planned for each of us. This undeniable friendship is from God. I pray that all women would have an Angelica and Erin to do life with. I wouldn't be who I am today without the prayers you pray, the truth you speak over me, the correction and rebuke that comes with grace and kindness, and most of all, the way you love my family and show up. Let's grow old together and never retire from doing the will of God in our lives. I'll cheer you on until the day I die, and then I'll cheer you on from above. You girls mean the world to me.

Bob Goff, Shontell Brewer, and Rita, you've helped me with every step of this writing project. I completed this book because of the inspiration, coaching, and editing you've provided. Thank you for believing in me. Thank you for taking time away from the important work you're doing to come alongside me and make this dream a reality.

xHope Staff and board members, thank you for empowering me and believing in me. I've learned so much doing ministry with each of you. The gifts and talents gathered in one room as we plan, prepare, and pray for the work we do at xHope each year is nothing short of God's beautiful example of the body of Christ at work for Kingdom impact.

Redeemer House Staff, students, and families, my Ugandan family, you are the why behind each and every mission trip. The redemption stories I've seen in your lives and families are proof that we are Not Forgotten. Someday I hope to write about your stories as I have our very own. God shines bright as you continue to share Jesus with the community, provide a home to orphans, educate vulnerable children, and lead people to Jesus. I'm honored to be loved by all of you. I'm the one who is forever changed because of the demonstration of Jesus I see every time I'm with you.

Bible study Babes and my Titus 2 mentors, you've become hype girls in my life, the kind of hype girls I've always prayed for. Studying the word with you ladies weekly, praying daily for one another, and sending words of encouragement and praise reports throughout the week is a catalyst to finish strong in our faith. We can do all things through Christ who gives us strength, And my favorite day of the week is gathering our husbands for couples bible studies. There is nothing more attractive than our men studying the word and growing in Jesus with us. Hallelujah, we have some amazing husbands to thank God for.

Thank you to my nieces and nephews, the ones who call me "auntie." Abby, Coleman, Charlie, Cienna, Tay, Kolton, Paitlee, Billy, Kai, Jeffrey, Molly, and Ellie. I've loved every season of life with you. From toddler to teenager to adulting, we have journeyed this road together. The trips to Uganda on mission, the sporting events, the vacations, and the many late-night chats, prayers, and Bible studies. I couldn't be prouder to see each of you living your lives for Jesus. I want you to always know that you are Not Forgotten by God, and that Auntie will always show up for you. I'm here. I'm available. Auntie loves you.

ABOUT THE AUTHOR

Wendi Cross is the cofounder and director of xHope, and Redeemer House Ministries in Uganda, a nonprofit ministry dedicated to the rescue, rehabilitation, and reunification of children into forever families.

Wendi and her husband, Rick, have six children, including two adopted sons, one from Africa and one through Sacramento County. They also have two daughters-in-law and three grandchildren. Wendi visits Redeemer House Children's Home in Uganda almost quarterly to oversee and work with the international ministries of xHope, known as Redeemer House Ministries. As a missionary team lead, Wendi brings teams of six to fourteen to serve alongside her at Redeemer House Children's Home and Redeemer Academy.

Wendi, a former elementary school teacher, earned her bachelor's degree in education from the University of Nevada Reno where she cheered four years on scholarship, served as a national cheer judge, and an ESPN2 announcer.

Wendi speaks and has spoken at school assemblies, Good Day Sacramento, Studio Live, ESPN2, live radio interviews, Rotary Clubs, Bible Study groups, adoption and foster care groups, Moms groups, Chamber events, various women's events, NFL holiday dinners, youth conferences, national conferences, and a variety of church services.

Whether speaking or writing, Wendi shares with transparency, inspiring others to make a difference one child and family at a time, beginning at home and expanding across the street and across the seas. Wendi's words will cheer you on in life and love. Once a cheerleader, always a cheerleader. To book Wendi for a speaking engagement, visit http://wendicross.com or send an email: wendi@ xhopemissions.org.